How to Open & Operate a Financially Successful

Wedding Consultant Business

With Companion CD-ROM

By John Peragine, Jr.

How to Open & Operate a Financially Successful Wedding Consultant & Planning Business —
With Companion CD-ROM

ISBN-13: 978-1-60138-114-9   ISBN-10: 1-60138-114-X

Library of Congress Cataloging-in-Publication Data
Peragine, John N., 1970-
  How to open & operate a financially successful wedding consultant & planning business :
(with companion CD-Rom) / by John N. Peragine, Jr.
     p. cm.
  Includes bibliographical references and index.
  ISBN-13: 978-1-60138-114-9 (alk. paper)
  ISBN-10: 1-60138-114-X (alk. paper)
 1. Wedding supplies and services industry--Management. 2. Consulting firms--Management.
3. New business enterprises--Management. I. Title. II. Title: How to open and operate a
financially successful wedding consultant and planning business.

  HD9999.W372P47 2008
  395.2'2068--dc22
                        2008008197

INTERIOR LAYOUT DESIGN: Vickie Taylor

Printed in the United States

Printed on Recycled Paper

A few years back we lost our beloved pet dog Bear, who was not only our best and dearest friend but also the "Vice President of Sunshine" here at Atlantic Publishing. He did not receive a salary but worked tirelessly 24 hours a day to please his parents.

Bear was a rescue dog who turned around and showered myself, my wife, Sherri, his grandparents Jean, Bob, and Nancy, and every person and animal he met (well, maybe not rabbits) with friendship and love. He made a lot of people smile every day.

We wanted you to know a portion of the profits of this book will be donated in Bear's memory to local animal shelters, parks, conservation organizations, and other individuals and nonprofit organizations in need of assistance.

– *Douglas & Sherri Brown*

PS: We have since adopted two more rescue dogs: first Scout, and the following year, Ginger. They were both mixed golden retrievers who needed a home.

Want to help animals and the world? Here are a dozen easy suggestions you and your family can implement today:

- *Adopt and rescue a pet from a local shelter.*
- *Support local and no-kill animal shelters.*
- *Plant a tree to honor someone you love.*
- *Be a developer — put up some birdhouses.*
- *Buy live, potted Christmas trees and replant them.*
- *Make sure you spend time with your animals each day.*
- *Save natural resources by recycling and buying recycled products.*
- *Drink tap water, or filter your own water at home.*
- *Whenever possible, limit your use of or do not use pesticides.*
- *If you eat seafood, make sustainable choices.*
- *Support your local farmers market.*
- *Get outside. Visit a park, volunteer, walk your dog, or ride your bike.*

Five years ago, Atlantic Publishing signed the Green Press Initiative. These guidelines promote environmentally friendly practices, such as using recycled stock and vegetable-based inks, avoiding waste, choosing energy-efficient resources, and promoting a no-pulping policy. We now use 100-percent recycled stock on all our books. The results: in one year, switching to post-consumer recycled stock saved 24 mature trees, 5,000 gallons of water, the equivalent of the total energy used for one home in a year, and the equivalent of the greenhouse gases from one car driven for a year.

Dedication

Author

*I dedicate this book to my beautiful wife, Kate, and my
shining daughters, Sarah and Loreena.*

*I also want to give a special thanks to my friends at the
Spilled Bean Coffee Shop who feed me coffee, one soup bowl
cup at a time.*

Contents

Table of

Dedication...3

Foreword...17

Introduction...21

Chapter 1: Pros & Cons of Opening a Consultant Business...23

Skills Needed to Be Successful...25

Jumping In and Getting Started...33

Characteristics of a Successful Consultant...34

Can I Make a Living as a Wedding Consultant?...37

History of Wedding Consulting as a Business...39

Where Can I Find Clients?...40

Internet 42

Advertising 44

Wedding Shows and Bridal Fairs 44

Word of Mouth 44

Be Recognized as a Professional 44

Initial and Ongoing Costs 45

What Kind of Personality Do I Need for Success? 49

Is This for Me? 50

What If I Have Never Been in Business Before? 51

Tried & True Success Methods of Consulting 52

Chapter 2: Home / Web-Based Consulting 55

Research on the Consulting Industry 55

Primary Research 55

Telephone Interviews 56

Face-to-Face Interviews 56

The Internet 56

Mail Survey 56

Mystery Shopping 58

Secondary Research 59

Understanding Your Competition 60

Competition 61

New Wedding Trends and Fashion 62

Entry Barriers...62

Exit Barriers 63

Teaming With Others 63

Bridal Shows 64

Who Is My Target Audience/Main Client Source?...........66

Will I Need a Lot of Money to Work From Home?...........68

Can I Work Strictly From Home?................................68

How Much Travel Is Involved? 69

What About Liability Insurance? 74

Types of Business Liability Insurance 74

Competing Venues/Business Owners............................76

Learning How to Work Independently..........................78

Chapter 3: A Business Plan: What Is It & Do I Need One? 81

Executive Summary...83

Objective 84

Mission 84

Keys to Success 84

Company Summary 84

Company Ownership 85

Start-Up Summary 85

Company Locations and Facilities 85

Services 85

Market Analysis Summary 87

Market Segmentation 88

Market Analysis 90

Target Market Segment Strategy 91

Market Needs 92

Service Business Analysis 92

Competition and Buying Patterns 92

Strategy and Implementation Summary 93

Competitive Edge 93

Sales Strategy 93

The Top Seven Suggestions for New Wedding Consultants 94

Initial Start-Up Costs 101

Operations.. 101

Consultations 103

The Wedding Day 103

Mistakes to Avoid 104

Strategies for Successful Consulting 105

The Wedding Industry and You 107

Licenses and Training Involved 109

Involving Your Community 111

Advertising.... 113

Newsletters.. 114

Brochures.... 115

Blogs.......... 116

Magazines and Newspapers 117

Mass E-mails 118

Bridal Shows 118

A CD Can Generate Business... 123

An Attendance List Is a Gold Mine 125

Comparison of Brick-and-Mortar Versus Home-Based.................. 126

Chapter 4: Wedding Packages & Options 129

Networking Opportunities 131

Exposure —Local and Nationwide 132

Conducting Business Legally 133

Conducting Business Ethically 134

Business Logo 134

Promotions 135

Chapter 5: IRS 137

Business Permits and Licenses 137

What Is a Federal ID Number? Do I Need One? 138

The IRS as Your Tax Information Source 139

Self-Employment Tax 140

Accounting Issues 141

Outside Vendors and How They Can Help 142

Confidentiality Issues 146

Desktop Programs That Can Help 146

Filing Taxes as a Business 147

Is Your Wedding Consulting a Business or a Hobby? 147

Depreciation 149

Avoiding an Audit 150

When to Hire an Accountant 151

Record Keeping 152

What Supplies/Forms Do I Need on Hand? 154

Chapter 6: What's in a Name 161
Choosing a Name for Your Business 161

Researching Availability of Names 162

Service Contracts 163

Rights of the Parties 169

Services Provided to Client 171

Chapter 7: Marketing 173
Setting Up Your Web Site 177

Driving Business to Your Web Site 178

Importance of a Home Page 178

Becoming Google Friendly 179

Should I Do It Myself or Hire Someone? 179

Business Cards 180

Chapter 8: Standard Operating Procedures *181*

Evaluating Your Success After Six Months 181

How to Do a SWOT Analysis 182

SWOT Worksheet — Strengths 182

SWOT Worksheet — Weaknesses 184

SWOT Worksheet — Opportunities 186

SWOT Worksheet — Threats 187

Surveys 188

How to Look at Success After One Year 191

Comparing Costs to Profits at the One-, Three-, and Five-Year Marks 192

Break-Even Analysis 192

Projected Profit and Loss 193

Profit Monthly 194

Profit Yearly 194

Gross Margin Monthly 195

Gross Margin Yearly 196

Projected Cash Flow 197

Cash Flow 197

Travel Costs for In-Person Events 198

Scheduling.. 199

Hired Help.. 200

Management Summary 206

Personnel Plan 207

End-of-the-Year Financial Analysis 207

How to Assess Success 210

Ongoing Generation of New Clients.................................. 211

Keeping Productivity on the Upswing 212

Chapter 9: The Psychology Behind Consulting 215

Why It Works 215

Correlations With Success 216

Personality Types and Success 216

Dos of Consulting... 217

Don'ts of Consulting 217

What If I Do Not Like a Client Personally?........................ 218

Having a Bad Day.. 219

Personality Traits That Can Harm Business 219

Chapter 10: Case Studies...................*221*

Appendix A: State Bridal Shows...*245*

XYZ Wedding Consultants' 255

Business Plan...255

Appendix B: Business Plan Sample.. *255*

Executive Summary..255

Objectives 256

Mission 256

Keys to Success 256

Company Summary 257

Company Ownership..257

Start-Up Summary 257

Company Locations and Facilities 259

Services 259

Market Analysis Summary...259

Market Segmentation 260

Target Market Segment Strategy 262

Market Needs...262

Service Business Analysis 263

Competition and Buying Patterns 263

Strategy and Implementation Summary 264

Competitive Edge..264

Sales Strategy 265

Management Summary 266

Personnel Plan...266

Financial Plan..267

Break-Even Analysis 267

Projected Profit and Loss 268

Projected Cash Flow......................................270

Appendix C: The Menu...................*273*

Appendix D: Seating Arrangements...*277*

Bibliography.....................................*281*

Biography *283*

Index *285*

Foreword

By Nikki Khan

Wedding consultants play an important role in making dream weddings come to life. From selecting photographers and florists to making the bride feel as comfortable as possible throughout the wedding planning process right up until the minute she walks down the aisle, wedding consultants do it all and must be willing to devote as much time as necessary to making sure that each and every detail is perfect on the big day.

Owning your own wedding consulting business is more than dealing with the minute details of planning and orchestrating a successful wedding event. Owning any type of business requires knowledge of bookkeeping, marketing, tax law, and finances, among other things. Running a wedding consultant business is no different. Owners must have a working knowledge of the operational and business aspects of their company as well as designing the reception space layout and providing the latest trends in wedding styles and fashion to the client.

John Peragine, in How to Open & Operate a Financially Successful Wedding Consultant Business, lays it all out for anyone thinking of opening a wedding consultant business. He begins by giving you an introduction into the business, providing readers with invaluable information on the personality characteristics of successful consultants and a realistic look at start-up costs involved with opening a wedding-planning business.

Having been in the wedding consulting business for over ten years, I can honestly say that this book is an excellent resource for new business owners. Peragine has provided a complete sample business plan, something that all new owners should invest time in if they want their business to run successfully for many years to come. Networking is essential in the wedding-planning business. The majority of your clients will be referred to you by former clients. Peragine offers a wealth of information on ways for you to get your business name out into the community, from word-of-mouth marketing to how to get your business featured in local and national newspapers and magazines.

As a wedding consultant, it is inevitable that you will come across a bride that may be more difficult to please. The author provides an entire chapter on the psychology behind the consulting business. He offers tips on how to handle even the most difficult of clients and how to get the job done successfully even if your personality clashes with a current client. Peragine makes your transition into business ownership easier by providing sample market analysis worksheets, press releases, contracts, and profit and loss statements, along with menus and seating arrangements that will help you jump right into the actual planning action.

The information provided in this book is extremely helpful. The tips and tricks that Peragine offers throughout are useful for anyone looking to open a wedding consultant business. Even seasoned business owners, such as myself, can use the invaluable information provided to better operate their businesses. With How to Open & Operate a Financially Successful Wedding Consultant Business, you can expect to receive new and fresh ideas on how to successfully jump into the wedding-planning business. Good luck on your journey toward business ownership and congratulations on taking the first steps in starting a career in the exciting world of wedding consulting.

Nikki Khan has been producing lavish and glamorous weddings and events in the greater Southern California area for over ten years. Before starting her own company, she worked for a large event production company. She has worked with numerous organizations including the Pacific Asia Museum, Paramount Studios, and has fostered extensive and lasting relationships with top tier suppliers in the wedding and event planning industry. Nikki provides fresh and innovative ideas for each occasion and always incorporates her clienteles' personal taste and style to each event. Her professionalism and relaxed demeanor has won accolades from her growing clientele.

She attended UCLA University and Swiss Finishing School and speaks numerous languages.

Nikki Khan
Exquisite Events
5635 Hazelcrest Circle
Westlake Village, CA 91362
Phone: 818-620-2665
Fax: 818-879-9115
Email: nikki@exquisevents.com
Web Page: **www.exquisevents.com**

Introduction

So do you think you have what it takes to be a wedding consultant? Can you match every kind of the color blue, repair hems with your eyes closed, and create fantasies out of flower arrangements? Creating a dream wedding requires imagination and energy, a concern for detail, and a love of organization to make certain that things run smoothly.

You will help couples decide on a budget and help them stick to it. You will also help them select the wedding dress; set trial hair and makeup appointments; confirm wedding day appointments; prepare and confirm wedding reception toasts or speeches; update life, house, and car insurance policies; complete change-of-name and change-of-address paperwork; open joint bank accounts; determine who will return the groom's formal attire; and arrange for a location, caterer, entertainment, wedding cake, and "going away" wardrobe. You will prepare for and run a successful wedding, including determining realistic costs, helping with the guest list, setting the wedding date, organizing the wedding ceremony and the reception, acquiring bridesmaids' and groom's attire, ordering invitations and other stationery, and dealing with the gifts and thank-you messages.

It takes more than just being able to run and plan a wedding. Wedding consulting is a business and it takes knowledge and skills to run a successful wedding consulting company. This book is packed full of everything you will need to become the most financially successful wedding consultant you can be.

Pros & Cons of
Opening a Consultant
Business

Chapter 1

Weddings are a multimillion-dollar business. In 2006, the Fairchild Bridal Group estimated that about $125 million was spent on about 2.1 million weddings. The cost of weddings, like many other things, has inflated drastically over the years. In the past, just the bride's family funded events. Now it is the bride, groom, and both of their families. That is as many as six wage earners as opposed to relying on the wage of the bride's father.

There has been a 73 percent increase in the cost of a wedding in the past 15 years according to the Fairchild Bridal Group. They estimate that the average cost of a wedding is now about $30,000. The bridal industry now encompasses a greater venue than it used to. It includes travel, home decorations, home furnishings, and much more.

The Fairchild Bridal Group estimates that the average age of couples getting married is 27 to 29. The average couples are older than they were 15 years ago. People are waiting longer to tie the knot. They have better jobs and know what they want more so than their younger counterparts do. They are willing to spend whatever it takes to get what they want, even if they go over their budget. In most cases, couples will spend much more than they originally budgeted.

The responsibility of who is paying the bill has also changed over the years. Since couples are older, they often are expected to pay their fair share. In

2007, about 25 percent of brides asked their mother and father to help pay for the wedding. About 30 percent of brides and grooms paid for the entire wedding on their own.

What does this all mean for a wedding consultant? It means that the field and the demand are growing. In addition, many more brides are choosing consultants to help them with their weddings. Since brides are older, many have full-time jobs, and they cannot spend the time that their younger counterparts could on planning and executing a wedding.

You can earn a good amount of money planning and executing weddings and parties. How much money? The average charge for a wedding consultant is usually based upon a percentage of the entire wedding cost — typically 10 to 15 percent. As a result, an average wedding consultant that does about ten weddings a year can make about $18,000 to $27,000 a year. You could do that on a part-time basis. If you intend to make it a full-time business of about 40 weddings a year, you could gross upwards of $70,000 a year.

However, there are drawbacks. Where you live can determine the amount of money you can expect to make. In New York and California the average wedding costs about $40,000; this is about $10,000 more than the national average. If you do not live in a metropolitan area, you could have a hard time making a living at wedding consulting. This does not mean you should give up your dream; this means you need to be creative and, at the same time, realistic.

Many wedding consultants work from home. This can be a blessing and a curse. If you are not a self-starter and motivated to work hard and market yourself, being at home can be a huge distraction. Wedding consulting is hard work because it is not just about planning a wedding reception and picking out flowers. It is about contracts, business, accounting, and negotiation.

Realistically, it can take a couple of years to be able to get a wedding consulting business off the ground. So do not quit your day job yet. You have to build a reputation and client base. Wedding consulting is not a business of repeat customers. Rather, it is a business built on word of mouth. Once you are successful at creating dreams for a bride, she will soon tell all of her friends to hire you right away. If a wedding does not go as well as everyone had hoped, then it can definitely hurt your ability to book future weddings.

Let me end this section on a high note. Wedding consulting is a very rewarding business because you are able to transform a couple's dreams into reality. Many women will say that they had their weddings planned out since they were a little girl. With your skills, contacts, and experience, you can make a fairy tale come true. Here are some other statistics from the Fairchild Bridal Group:

- ♥ This year, it is estimated that 1 out of 64 women in the United States got married.

- ♥ This year there will be about 42,300 weddings every weekend in the United States.

- ♥ This year, there will be about 17 million bridesmaids and groomsmen.

- ♥ Finally, this year there will be about 287 million wedding guests.

Each of these people could need your help as a consultant. Each of these couples is willing to pay you an average of $3,000 to $4,500 to assist with the wedding plans. Each guest and member of the wedding party could be your next client. The wedding consulting business is viable and growing. All you need are the skills and know-how to be the next successful consultant.

Skills Needed to Be Successful

One of the more important skills to have is a sense of humor. Murphy's Law is often in effect when planning a wedding.

*Murphy's Law states things will go
wrong in any given situation, if you
give them a chance.*

There are all sorts of emergencies that can arise during the planning of a wedding. The caterer may quit or a band may not show up. A wedding consultant must be flexible and maintain that sense of humor in the face of adversity. If not, he or she could lose her cool and in turn, lose future clients. Having a sense of humor is not making light of a situation; it means that you have a positive way to deal with stress as it comes.

Weddings can be awkward times for families. Mothers and fathers are losing their children, and at the same time they are combining their family with strangers. Having a sense a humor can serve to diffuse that stress and discomfort. Laughter can be truly the best medicine at a wedding rehearsal.

You have to like dealing with people. You will be a bride's best friend, worst enemy, confidant, and counselor all rolled up in one. It will be the rare occasion that you will not have plenty of Kleenex on hand as the bride cries and becomes upset.

Being a great listener is an essential trait in wedding consultants. They must listen carefully as the bride and the families describe what they want in their wedding. If you do not have active listening skills, you may miss an important feature, such as they wanted blue ribbons on the table, not pink. Making a mistake because you were not listening can be costly.

Here is a list of different traits and skills that make a great wedding consultant:

- Persistence

- The ability to coordinate and consolidate resources

- A strong desire to succeed

💜 Independent personality

💜 Commitment to the client and the work

💜 A vision for the wedding and your business

💜 A sense of competitiveness and drive to succeed over other consultants

💜 Luck — there is a certain amount of luck in any business

💜 Personal initiative and desire to strive for excellence

💜 A high energy level — you will need this in every aspect of wedding consulting.

💜 Desire for immediate feedback — you want to be able to transfer the feedback into excellence.

💜 A demanding nature — you must demand that vendors produce what they promise and demand excellence in yourself.

💜 Creativity

💜 Strong integrity — this is based on honesty and the ability to produce what you promise

💜 Good at calculated risk taking — there is a certain amount of risk and you must know your limit and have the ability to calculate whether the risk is worth taking.

💜 Tolerance for ambiguity — sometimes others are not clear and do not communicate well. You must be able to ask questions and clarify things you do not understand and be tolerant of others that lack good communication skills.

💜 A desire to work hard — this is a hard job, and you must be willing to work hard every day in everything you do.

♥ You must have a high tolerance for failure. You will not always succeed. Mistakes are an opportunity to learn. If you have a low tolerance and are prone to fits, this may not be the business venture for you.

♥ A sense of inquisitiveness

♥ Goal-oriented behavior — everything you do will need to be taking steps toward your personal goals and the goals of your client. If you get off track, you must be able to get back on track quickly.

♥ Self-confidence — If you do not believe in yourself and your abilities, no one else will either.

♥ Innovative thinking — You must think of new ways to do things. Fashion and style change constantly. You need to be able to breathe life into an old idea.

♥ Problem-solving skills — There will be challenges you will face constantly for which you will need to have good problem-solving skills to fix quickly and successfully.

♥ High reliability and dependability.

♥ Strong management and organizational skills — This book was created upon the fundamental concept that wedding consulting is a business. If you cannot manage others and you are not organized, you will not succeed very long. Look at your house and car and be honest. Are you really organized and detail oriented?

You also need the above-mentioned skills with vendors and other businesses that you will need to deal with. Being able to listen and repeat back what is said is important in business dealings, as it can erase most misunderstandings later. It is always easier to get something right the first time than to have to go back in and fix it later. In business dealings, you must listen carefully to what the costs of things are. If you do not listen and clarify items in the beginning, you could find yourself arguing about a huge bill at the end.

Patience is another important skill, as weddings are a time of high stress. As things progress, a bride may make changes to her original plan. Stress can make people act differently than they normally do. Having patience can help talk a wild-eyed bride down from borderline homicidal tendencies.

Being creative and artistic is important if you want to become a wedding consultant. Having an eye for color, design, and flair all play into making a wedding a memorable experience. The ability to translate what the bride has in her mind is a special skill. Being creative and finding the right materials and items to make that vision shine is something you are born with, and can be refined with practice and experience.

You have to have some theatrics in your blood. You are putting on a show. It is a one-time engagement and so it has to be right the first time. Unlike other shows, this one usually has only one rehearsal. It will have grand costumes and sets. There will be food and other entertainment to keep the audience fed and entertained. You are the director. The wedding party and person presiding over the ceremony are your actors. There will be music, movement, lines to say, and in some cases, special effects. You have to know how to direct people and be able to get them to do it right the first time. This is an essential trait or the whole show can be a bomb.

The difference between a party planner and a successful wedding consultant has to do somewhat with artistic vision and the ability to coordinate colors, but to be great you must have some business savvy. That is where this book will benefit you. It will help you take that step from average to great.

A wedding coordinator is hired because of his or her knowledge about how to set up and run a wedding from start to finish. This includes knowing wedding etiquette, knowing the right people in the business of weddings, and being able to translate a bride's vision. All of this is done with flair, within the family's stated budget.

Successful wedding consultants need to be experts in many different aspects, including hospitality, event planning, decorating, and wedding trends. They need to have knowledge about different wedding practices and traditions. A wedding consultant has a finger on the pulse of the latest trends in wedding products and services, food, music, ceremony, and reception decorations and design.

Wedding consultants have to have an above-average fashion sense. They will need to know all the current fashion trends and where to find these fashions. In addition to the wedding dress, they will need to know about wedding party fashions including bridesmaids and parents. This fashion sense needs to reach to men's fashions for the groom and his groomsmen. The days of just putting on your father's suit to be "hitched" are passé. There are so many accessories to keep up with, such as headpieces, veils, shoes, and gloves. A wedding consultant must know where to get good alterations quickly and on a moment's notice. There will be that time when a bride has lost thirty pounds since her fitting and a dress needs to be altered overnight. A wedding consultant will know just whom to call.

In addition to what you know, whom you know is equally important. You need to know:

- Caterers

- Hotel clerks

- Photographers

- Musicians

- Designers

- Cake decorators

- Seamstresses to do alternations

- Venue renters

- Tuxedo renters

- Wedding dress makers

- Party supply renters

- Videographers

- Florists

- Ministers

- Jewelers

- Notaries

- Church directors

- Travel agents

- Any other person involved in wedding services

You must have good networks and possess good contacts with high-quality, reliable wedding services. You need to know how to negotiate with these goods and services providers and be able to coordinate all of these services during the wedding. It can be quite a juggling act.

If you think you have what it takes, take the wedding consultant quiz.

♡ WEDDING CONSULTANT QUIZ ♡	Yes	No
1. Do you laugh in times of stress?		
2. Do you know what colors can coordinate with the color pink?		

♡ WEDDING CONSULTANT QUIZ ♡	Yes	No
3. Can you get in front of a group of people and get their attention? (Imagine about 100 people all talking at once and you need to tell them where to line up for food.)		
4. Are you a flexible person?		
5. Do you admit that it is the couple's day and not yours?		
6. Are you a self-starter?		
7. Can you bargain shop?		
8. Do you have contacts in the wedding field? (Music, food, venues, and so on.)		
9. Can you make a decision and stick by it when you know it is right?		
10. Can you take a break when you need a break?		
11. Are you a good listener?		
12. Are you artistic?		
13. Do you know fashion dos and don'ts?		
14. Do you know how to tell if it is going to rain?		
15. Have you enough savvy to save money for dry spells?		
16. Do you know a few good jokes? (Clean and dirty?)		
17. Can you dance? (Even a conga line counts.)		
18. Can you think ahead and make sure every detail is covered?		
19. Can you handle a bride when she is crying and ready to fall apart?		
20. Do you always carry extra Kleenex and headache medicine?		

If you answered yes to 15 to 20 questions, then you are well on your way to becoming a wedding consultant.

10 to 15 = You need to brush up on some of your skills, but there is still hope for you to become a successful wedding consultant.

6 to 9 = You need a lot of work if you hope to make it as a wedding consultant.

0 to 5 = You might want to see if a local fast food restaurant is hiring for children's birthday parties.

Jumping In and Getting Started

If you made it past the quiz, the next thing to do is to assess what you need to do next, and you have a few options. One is to find another consultant and try to work under her or him for a while. You will be able to learn the ropes and start to make contacts. You will truly find out what hard work the job involves, and you will discover how rewarding it can be. If you are lucky enough to find someone to apprentice with, make sure you ask tons of questions. Carry a small notebook with you to make notes and to write down contacts. This can be invaluable to you later.

The following are tips that can help you start your wedding consulting business on the right foot:

1. Here is a trick you can use to give your clients the impression that you have an office outside of your home: You can check around and see if you can rent an office by the hour. You give the illusion when you meet with your clients that you have an office. You can also look into other meeting spaces that you can rent when meeting prospective clients.

2. Why not use technology to make you look more professional? You can find a company to answer your phone. These services are sometimes known as virtual secretaries. Instead of your client calling and talking to an answering machine, they can talk to a real person. Many times if potential clients reach a machine they are likely to hang up and call the next number to talk with a live person. A virtual assistant can solve this problem. They answer the phone 24 hours a day, seven days a week. Instead of your clients imagining you at home doing business in your back room, they will imagine a professional office with a secretary. Virtual secretaries can make and keep up with your appointments, and answer common questions a client may have. This service can cost around $40 a month.

3. One thing that young people in college need is extra cash. This is especially true of college interns. They often have to do their

internship without any compensation. Hiring an intern can be a great idea, and it can help both of you. Interns can do small tasks while you concentrate on the bigger items that need to be attended to as a wedding consultant. Your intern can do errands, set up tables and other decorations, keep up with your appointments, answer the phone, make copies, or any other task that can take you away from focusing on the wedding. Depending on their expertise, they can help with your Internet Web page, public relations, or answering clients' questions. They can even keep children busy when you are trying to get a wedding rehearsal underway. The possibilities are endless.

4. Have you considered asking friends and family to help you? Your immediate support network can really help you out with your wedding consulting business. You cannot do everything yourself, and you should not try to. If you try to handle everything by yourself, you will burn out and the quality of your work and service can suffer. Ask for help when you need it.

5. Ask for feedback from family and friends. They know you best and can be honest with you. You can trust their advice because they want you to succeed. They will be open and give you feedback about how to make your business better, and they can provide you with motivation and support. They will be your cheering section and your best critics. Best of all, the valuable service they provide will be free, so be sure to thank them.

Characteristics of a Successful Consultant

Here is a list of questions and qualities about which you need to do some soul searching. Do you possess any of them? Successful entrepreneurs, and especially wedding consultants, must possess these traits:

♥ Are you a self-starter or do you have to be told what to do? As a wedding consultant, you must have the ability to create weddings from start to finish and coordinate each step to make it happen.

♥ Do you have the ability to get along with different personalities? You have to be able to develop business relationships and working relationships with a variety of different people and different personalities. You will be dealing with brides, grooms, families, friends, and vendors of many different types. How well can you deal with a client that demands a lot? It is not a matter of "if" you will encounter a difficult client; it is more fair to say "when" and "how many" difficult clients you will have to deal with. Will you have the patience and stamina to deal with them?

♥ What are your decision-making skills? As a wedding consultant, you will have to make decisions constantly and quickly. Are you the type of person that needs time to mull a decision over, or can you make decisions on the fly? Can you make decisions under pressure and independently?

♥ Being a wedding consultant can be a very tiring and physically demanding business. Expect to have some sleepless nights. It is exciting to own your own wedding consulting business but it is also a lot of hard work. Can you work six or seven days a week to get the job done? Does your life allow you to work these extended hours?

♥ Do you have good organizational skills? Poor planning is one of the main reasons that wedding consultant businesses fail. If you are a good organizer, it can help you with the day-to-day duties of a wedding consultant, but it can also help you keep up with the financial part of your business.

♥ Do you have the passion to be a wedding consultant? If you are in the field because you think it is an easy way to make money, then you chance for success may be slim. If you are passionate about what you are doing and are motivated, then you have what it takes to succeed. When times get tough, your motivation can help pull you through. If your heart is not truly in the business, you are more likely to give up and quit. You can also experience burnout and experience negative feelings and emotions. If you are truly passionate, you will look forward to working as a consultant each day and this passion will show through in everything you do. Your passion will be contagious.

♥ What does your family think about your decision to become a wedding consultant? You will have to give up your time to make the business work. Is your family supportive and behind your decision? If you cannot rely on their support, you will not survive very long. You will be torn and your family will win out most of the time. If they are willing to support you, that support can bolster you. They must understand that in addition to giving up your time you may also create a strain on the finances. Is everyone willing to cut back their spending to help you through the beginning stages of your dream? It can take months or years before you will see a substantial profit from your endeavors. This could mean you have to change your standard of living. Is your family willing to downsize?

♥ Do you have business goals? We will discuss mission statements and a business plan throughout this book. What are your long- and short-term goals? Does being a wedding consultant fit into the other plans you had for yourself in other areas of your life (marriage, family, finances, spiritual, and so on)? Your goals will define the type of consulting business you will have. Will it be a destination wedding consulting business where you get to travel? Will it be a high-end clientele business where you will hobnob with famous and influential people? Will it be a down-home low-key wedding consulting business created for women on a budget? You need to decide what your goals are for your business and make sure what you create is what you truly want.

One of the defining aspects of successful consultants is their business sense. You will need to develop a business plan early on and figure out what your expenses will be and stick to your budget. If you want to be able to keep the lights on at home, you will need to learn how to market yourself and when you get a little extra money you will need to learn to save.

You can have the best fashion sense and be able to throw legendary parties, but without a good solid business sense, you will not survive very long.

Included in this book and its accompanying CD is a business plan. This is a great template to work from to create your own business plan. It is a living, breathing document that will need to adjust as your business grows. It should be consulted on a regular basis and adjusted to meet your needs.

You have to be diligent about your expenses and fees. If you pay vendors on time, they will be loyal and cut you breaks in the future. Stay on top of outstanding bills. Do not allow families to talk you into cutting your prices. This is a business, so if you want to give people a break, then you should consider doing wedding consulting as a hobby rather than a full-time job. If you cut your rates in order to get more jobs, then your clients will expect this rate in future jobs. Set a reasonable price and stick to it.

Characteristically a successful wedding consultant is a person that is organized. Look around you. If your life and home are a wreck, how do you expect to organize other people's events? You have to make sure you do not miss a detail. You have to be able to look into the future and anticipate every contingency.

Successful wedding consultants are calm and confident. They know their business and stay up on the current trends. They are professional at all times and always aim to please. If you are the type of person that is easily offended, then wedding consulting may not be your calling. Brides, grooms, and wedding families can act differently when under stress. Successful wedding consultants are not easily offended by insults and are open to criticism. This is just as much a part of the job as setting up rehearsal dinners and tea parties.

Can I Make a Living as a Wedding Consultant?

In order to be truly successful and make a living as a wedding consultant, there are certain elements that you may want to consider.

❤   Do you have a willingness to take on acceptable risks? If you have an aversion to risk taking, you will not be successful as a wedding consultant.

♥ Do you have what it takes in order to take on a smart, measured amount of risk? There are people who left their high-paying corporate jobs to become wedding consultants and are doing quite well. There are other wedding consultants that have quit their corporate jobs to be consultants and have done poorly. If you are one of those people who can take on a risky project — or one that you have autonomy in — and are successful at it, then you should do well as a wedding consultant.

♥ Does the idea of sales intimidate you? Some people are not good at selling themselves or their service. If you cannot be a good sales clerk and are timid, you may not succeed as a wedding consultant. You have to believe in yourself and be able to sell the idea that your service is necessary and that you are the best person for the job.

♥ Do you have the ability to delegate tasks? You have to be a strong leader and be able to delegate certain tasks to others to get the job done. Without this skill, you might be overwhelmed and not be able to do everything that needs to be done. You have a schedule and you must be able to lead others and tell them what to do without apprehension.

As long as you keep an eye on the business side of wedding consulting, you can make a good living at it. You need to have reasonable expectations and a strong business sense. You have to devote time to marketing yourself, because while marketing may not pay money, it will generate money. You have to get your name and service out in the community. You cannot simply hang a shingle and expect people to begin knocking on your door immediately, begging you to create the wedding of their dreams.

Having a business background can help ensure that you make a living as a wedding consultant. In addition to being able to negotiate contracts, collect money, and pay vendors, there are personal business expenses and accounting that has to take place. You have to know how to balance a checkbook, maintain an account, and pay your taxes to the Internal Revenue Service (IRS). Knowing how to develop a budget and pay your expenses can go a long way in making sure you are successful as a consultant.

History of Wedding Consulting as a Business

The history of wedding consulting goes back centuries in many cultures. There has always been an elder person that families asked to arrange and conduct marriages. These "matchmakers" were called upon to make a good match and to coordinate a wedding. These were often full-time professions for certain members in these societies.

Sometimes, the duties of coordinating a wedding fell upon the mother of the bride. Weddings took place in the home rather than in churches and other venues. These weddings were usually done in families' backyards or living rooms. To have a wedding in a church or other large venue is a more modern invention. Sixty years ago, it was still common to have a marriage at home; only the wealthy could afford lavish weddings in churches.

Times changed as the role of women changed. Women went into the workforce. This includes many women that are now reaching retirement age. They did not have the time to sew a dress, cook all day, decorate a home, and make flower arrangements. These items have increasingly been taken over by caterers, decorators, dressmakers, and florists. As these parts of the wedding were taken out of the home and given over to professionals, families began to have difficulty coordinating all of these services to create a wedding. Weddings are now done more often outside the home. With parents, brides, grooms, and wedding parties all having full-time jobs and very little free time, a gap needed to be filled. Eventually this was done by wedding consultants. These consultants provide knowledge, experience, and contacts to make sure all of the services are provided and the vision of a wedding is created. People are willing to pay for this service because they frankly do not have the time or resources to do it themselves. A huge burden is lifted from a family when a well-seasoned wedding consultant can come in and take over all of the details. The brides do not have to take off weeks of work to get it done themselves, which saves time and money. In fact, weddings done with consultants can sometimes cost less. This is because consultants know where to find the best deals, and they have working relationships with many different vendors to get the best prices on wedding goods and services.

Where Can I Find Clients?

The obvious place to find clients are places where women are, and at venues for wedding goods and services. You will have to look for clients and not expect them to know you are in business just because you make business cards and may have set up a Web site. One thing you may want to consider is your desired demographics. With whom do you want to do business? This will determine the type of business you establish and where you do your marketing.

The definition of demographics is the characteristics of the people in your target audience. Demographics reveal who is more likely to use your services or products. Some of the characteristics you may want to consider are the age of people you are targeting, their income level, where they live, the types of weddings they might want, and their education level. These demographics will really define your business. You are looking for a niche or area that will make you an expert. In addition, when you determine your clients' demographics, you will then be able to determine where you need to start seeking them out.

One of the more important demographics to consider is age. As mentioned earlier in the chapter, brides are waiting later in life to get married. The average age is now 27 to 29. This demographic is important because if you are spending your time and effort on women in their early twenties, you may be wasting valuable time and resources. Once you have determined whether your age group is near you, then you can decide on a marketing strategy. If this age group is not present, you many need to rethink your business options. This does not mean that all is lost if there is not a large population of people in their late twenties. Parents still help pay for weddings, so your strategy may target them rather than the brides themselves.

You could decide that older brides will be the demographic that you will target. There are many women that are getting remarried in later life. Maybe when they were younger they wanted to be in control of every aspect of their wedding. Now, they might be relieved to place the wedding planning in hands that are more capable and relax a little. Things may have changed since their first marriage; they may have a career and children that take up most of their time. You can target your marketing toward that fact. That is why it is so imperative that you know the demographics of your potential clients.

Another demographic to consider is women with professions. They have three things that can work to your advantage:

1. They have the money to spend on a wedding and especially on a wedding consultant.

2. They do not have the time to make all of their arrangements because of time constraints imposed upon them by their job.

3. They know the value of outsourcing to professionals.

Professional women have the money due to having a career. This gives them the resources needed to create the wedding they have envisioned. They do not have to ask for money to help them create what they want; they are paying for it themselves. They have the extra cash it takes to hire a professional wedding planner.

Professional women do not have the extra time to spend planning a wedding. They have careers and do not want to give up precious time hunting down a caterer. They would rather have someone else do it for them. This can also translate to more money in your pocket. All-inclusive packages are the most expensive that wedding consultants can offer. Due to the time constraints, women with careers are more likely to buy these packages and have you do all the work.

Professional women become successful and can rise up the ladder of promotions because they know how to delegate jobs. They know when something needs to be done, and everyone is busy, that they may need to outsource certain projects to be completed on time. That is why it is so natural for them to hire wedding consultants to get the job done, so they do not have to worry.

Another demographic to consider is the economic one. This is important for a number of reasons. First, if you are trying to solicit work in an area that is predominately poor, you may be wasting your time. You have to keep in mind that wedding consulting is not a necessity for a wedding. People that have a middle-class and high income are the folks more likely to access your services.

The second thing about economics is that you want to be paid. If you want to do wedding consulting as a hobby and charity, that is fine. If you intend to make a living or get money for what you do, you have to consider whether the bride and groom can afford you. If you charge 10 percent of the entire wedding, your fee may look like this when a family budgets for a wedding:

$30,000 for the wedding plus $3,000 (10 percent) for your fee for a grand total of $33,000.

This may be the agreement up front. Now, let us suppose that the budget runs over and the wedding costs $45,000. With your fee, it brings the total to $49,500. That is $16,500 over budget. There is a good chance you will not be paid. So, be honest with a couple when you are developing a contract. More importantly, make sure the demographic you have chosen can afford your fees.

Once you have determined what your market is, here are some ways to begin generating some business.

Internet

One of the most powerful tools that has been invented for the home-based business is the Internet. It makes working at home realistic and affordable. Without the hassle of paying for and furnishing an office, you have more time to concentrate on wedding planning rather than how you will pay the overhead of rent. In Chapter 7, on marketing, we will discuss how to create a knockout Web site to generate business. The Internet allows you to hang your "virtual" shingle and drive customers to you.

"The top reason online consumers prefer to shop on the Web is to avoid crowds, a reason cited by 38 percent of respondents. The next four reasons consumers prefer the Web, and the percent of respondents citing them: Lower prices, 35 percent; ease of comparing products and prices, 28 percent; avoiding the inconvenience of traveling to stores, 28 percent; and a wider selection of products, 26 percent."

Nielsen/NetRatings, Goldman, Sachs & Co. and Harris Interactive 12/2003

You can create your own Web site for free using software available for download on the Internet. Here are few sites to consider:

- **http://www.personalwebkit.com/** — This site offers a simple Web design program for free. If you want the full version to create more than one site, then you have to pay a fee.

- **http://www.homestead.com/** — This site allows you to try their Web-building program for 30 days for free. They also offer Web-hosting services.

- **http://www.coffeecup.com/designer/** — This site offers a free shareware Web site creation program.

- **http://www.facebook.com/** — This is a great way to connect to people and advertise your service. You do not have to know how to design a Web site. They provide a template; you just fill in the information and it creates the page for you.

Advertising

A great way to get your name out there is to advertise. Without advertising your business, people will not know that you even exist. This has some start-up costs involved, but you can start simple and work your way toward a larger advertising budget. Some places to start advertising your business are local or national newspapers or bridal magazines. These will vary in price and will be discussed in more depth in Chapter 7. For now, consider a modest advertisement or a listing in the classified ads.

Wedding Shows and Bridal Fairs

Where do brides go to find bridal consultants? Wedding shows and bridal fairs. This is the place to show off your talent and the portfolio you have begun to create. These types of shows expose your work to a wider audience and give you an opportunity to meet and develop networks with vendors. Some shows will charge a fee for setting up a table or booth. Make sure you have plenty of business cards. In Chapter 7, we will discuss tricks to get people to notice you at these events.

Word of Mouth

Remember that word of mouth is your bread and butter. If you are just starting out then you may not have that many former clients. Even if you did cousin Kerry's wedding or Uncle Kris's reception, make sure you have them write recommendations for you. You more than likely did it for them for free, so they can at least help you out with a few kind words. In addition, encourage them to tell their friends about your service.

Be Recognized as a Professional

There are professional organizations both nationally and locally that you can join in order to help develop your wedding consulting skills, as well as make yourself look more professional. By joining a professional association, you will be able to keep up with new trends in the industry. Memberships can also allow you to network with other wedding planning service providers. You can also put your name on their advertising boards. When people are looking for professional wedding planners in their area, they will often go to a professional organization's Web site to find out what is available. Having your name and information on these sites can help increase your exposure. Clients are looking for professionals to take care of their special day, so they are looking at places where they can find the most highly qualified professionals. Being a member of these professional organizations can be very impressive to your clients, so make sure you include this information in your material and public relations (PR) materials.

Initial and Ongoing Costs

In Chapter 3, we will explore the cost of equipment and other incidental costs. Beginning a wedding consulting business can cost very little. As you will see in the sample business plan in Chapter 3, some money to begin your business will be included. This is the smartest way to start any business, especially if you are going from a full-time job with benefits to working for yourself. Having some money in the bank can help defray the initial costs that you may encounter. Here are some items to consider that will help you get started on the right foot:

- ♥ **Marketing costs** — (advertising, business cards, brochures)

- ♥ **Available cash on hand** — There may be times that you will need to pay for an item or a deposit to hold a venue or service. You will be paid later but you need to up-front money at times to pay for items. Make sure that these charges are included in your contract.

- ♥ **Income.** — As you are building your business, you will still have to pay your personal bills at home. Having money saved in the bank can help you pay your rent and electric bill until you start being paid. Consider that even if you were going to get a job today, it could be six months to a year before you are paid, depending on how far in advance a bride begins her wedding arrangements.

In the business plan found in Chapter 3, you will notice two important amounts. The first is the start-up costs and the second is start-up assets. Start-up costs consist of business equipment, stationery, and your initial marketing and PR. The start-up assets are what you have in the bank. This is the money to keep your business up and running. You will add to this as your business grows, but you will need some money to keep things afloat until you begin to get money from clients. Remember, today's client could mean a payday in a year.

So what are your options if you do not have start-up funds? Start-up funds are not essential, but without some sort of funds available, your dreams of being a successful wedding consultant can be short-lived. Here are some options to access the cash you need.

- ♥ **Go to your bank.** Ask for money the good old-fashioned way. Most banks still lend money for small businesses. If you have good credit, securing a loan should not be too much trouble. Make sure you look at the fine print, like the interest rate and any penalties for paying off the loan early. As your business grows, try to pay off your loan as quickly as possible. Once you have done this your bank may offer you a line a credit that can help you when times get rough or you want to expand.

- ♥ **Ask family and friends.** If you can ask more than one person for a small loan, you may be more successful than asking one person for a large loan. Make a written statement of how you intend to pay the loan back, interest, and when they can expect payments to begin. While friends and family can be more flexible and generous than a bank can be, it is not recommended you take advantage of that fact. You never know when you might need a few warm bodies in a pinch, so do not burn any bridges.

- ♥ **A Small Business Administration (SBA) microloan** is another way to secure cash. The main purpose of microloans is to provide small loans to individuals who are looking to start a small business of their own. To assist that process and prevent the individuals from being saddled with massive debt, the microloan program was created to lend a helping hand and get entrepreneurs on their way.

In the United States, the microloan program was created under the jurisdiction of the SBA to provide small loans to start-ups, newly established, or growing small business concerns. Through the program, funds are made available to nonprofit community-based lenders who provide the loans to eligible borrowers. The loans can be as high as $35,000, but often they are in the range of $13,000. The Microloan Program, not surprisingly, has proven to be immensely popular in the United States, providing billions of dollars every year to tens of thousands of entrepreneurs who are just trying to start out in their sector of business. When looking for a microloan member, make sure that the lender is registered with the SBA. Before you go to the lender, ensure that you will be able to repay the loan. A microlender is required by law to consider your ability to pay back the loan. If you can show them why you have thought it through, and how you will pay it back, it will make the entire process much, much easier.

♥ **Consider a peer-to-peer lending site**, such as **www.prosper.com**. This is good if your credit is not as good as you like and you are having difficulty securing a loan for your wedding consulting business. Prosper.com is a market that allows borrowers to request loans up to $25,000. Borrowers post a listing and state how much they want to borrow, why they want it and the maximum interest rate they want to pay. A lender can search these profiles and bid on lending some of the money requested. When the borrower gets enough lenders, they get the loan. The interest rate is based on factors such as credit score. The reason it is a good option is the people lending the money are not banks or financial institutions. They are people just like you that want to help others start a new business.

You will have ongoing expenses that you will need to keep a tally of and make sure that you have the resources to meet these costs. Here is a list of some common expenses:

♥ Travel

♥ Rent (even if it is at home)

♥ Telephone

♥ Internet

♥ Office supplies

♥ Marketing

♥ Advertising

♥ Stationery and cards

♥ Equipment replacement

♥ Upkeep of your transportation

♥ Parking and toll fees

♥ Business-related meals

♥ Special gifts for clients

♥ Expansion

♥ Insurance

♥ Education

♥ Trade shows (these can be very costly)

♥ Business and professional licenses

These are just a few of the expenses you may incur. You need to keep track of and make sure you are saving money for these expenses as they come up. It is not a matter of "if it happens"; it is better to think, "When it happens."

What Kind of Personality Do I Need for Success?

There are a few personality traits needed to become a successful wedding consultant.

1. **Extrovert** — You cannot be shy. You need to be outgoing be able to engage people. You need to light up a room when you enter; you should never outshine the bride, however. You must be able to look people in the eye when they are talking to you and introduce yourself immediately when someone new comes in the door. People must want to flock to you due to your bubbly and shining personality.

2. **Patience** — You must have an extremely high tolerance. If you are prone to get mad, frustrated, or fly off the handle, then this job is not for you. There will be times that things do not go as planned, like when the bride or her family may snap at you, or even the occasional wedding cake disaster. You must be able to laugh off these situations and move on to a solution. Things happen, and you must be prepared to deal with them all. That is why the family hired a professional, right?

3. **Confidence** — You must exude confidence from every part of your being. If you seem unsure about yourself or the wedding planning process, the bride and others can get very uneasy. They are relying on you to be the professional and take care of everything. If you present a sense of confidence, and things are going awry, the bride will have a level of comfort knowing that you are taking care of it properly.

4. **Sense of humor** — This can be one of the greatest personality traits to have. If you know how to relax clients through humor, the process will move along so much smoother. To have the ability to de-escalate a situation through laughter is truly a gift. If you

possess this gift, then wedding consulting may be the career for you.

5. **People person** — You have to really like people. You cannot fake it. People are savvy enough to know the difference. If people feel that you really care about them and their wedding, they will be knocking your door down. Wedding consulting is more than just a cold, impersonal business. It is about building positive relationships and rapport with your clients. You have to think beyond the current client and think about what kind of word-of-mouth business that they can generate for you.

Is This for Me?

Wedding consulting is not for everyone. If you commit all the time and effort it takes to become a successful wedding consultant and decide you really do not like it, then you will be miserable.

When you go to buy a car you do not usually go to a car lot, point at a car and say, "Let me have the keys, I am taking it home."

Most people want to test drive the car. Some people want to go home and sleep on it before they make a decision. A career decision such as becoming a wedding consultant is the same way. Test-drive it first.

Offer to do some wedding consulting for family and friends before taking the plunge and deciding it is what you want to do. If you watched the movie "The Wedding Planner," and liked the idea of the romantic notion of being a wedding planner, you might want to reconsider. You may find that you hate the stress, the periods of no work, and brides that are not always thankful for your presence. Trying out a couple weddings first is a good way to see if wedding consulting resonates with you.

The wedding consultants that are truly successful at what they do love their job and love the process from beginning to end. There are other similar jobs, such as event planning, that may be more to your liking. You still get to plan events, but you do not have to deal with all of the drama that weddings often have surrounding them. Some people thrive on the satisfaction that they are making someone else's dreams come true. Are you one of these people? You have to be the one to make that decision. If it is the right decision for you, then you will be rewarded every day.

What If I Have Never Been in Business Before?

Having experience in the wedding industry is an advantage, but it is not a necessity. Having the experience of running your own business is beneficial, but everyone starts somewhere.

Since you are just starting out on a new venture, one of the best things to do is to find someone that has already been down the same road for help. Luke Skywalker did not become a Jedi on his own, as he needed the help from Obi-Wan. Obi-Wan had the experience and knew the tricks and the pitfalls associated in becoming a Jedi knight.

Try to find your own Obi-Wan. This can be difficult sometimes, because wedding consulting can be such a competitive business and people do not want to create more competition. That is why some people join professional wedding consulting organizations or sign up for classes. This gives them access to those who have the experience and the answers to their questions.

Wedding consulting is not the type of career that takes years of training and multiple college degrees. It is as much an art as it is a science. Each wedding is different and presents its own unique challenges. Each wedding is like a painting. The picture you are creating is unique. It may need different colors, shades, and mediums to complete. When it is expertly executed, it is truly a masterpiece to behold.

This book should give you the answers to most of the questions that both novice and expert wedding consultants could have. If you feel that you do not have a firm grasp on the business side of wedding consulting and are worried you will do something wrong, you might want to consider taking a class in small business. Many times your local community college will offer these types of classes. They are often held on nights and weekends so that they can fit in your schedule and still allow you to raise a family and continue to grow your wedding consulting business.

If your schedule does not allow you to seek conventional education methods or there is not a school nearby, consider taking some courses online. Here are some sites to consider:

- **http://www.sba.gov/services/training/index.html** — This is a course created through the Small Business Association. The best part about these courses is that they are free.

- **http://www.remotecourse.com/Personal-Business.cfm** — This site offers a number of courses in small business. The price for the courses start at about $100.

- **http://www.microsoft.com/smallbusiness/small-business-plus/sign-up.aspx** — This site, sponsored by Microsoft, offers free courses in small business. You just have to sign up on their site, which is also free.

Tried & True Success Methods of Consulting

There are a couple of things you can do that will improve your success as a wedding consultant:

1. Get some experience running weddings or other large events by working with someone else.

2. Start small, think big. You should start out on your own or with someone that has experience as a wedding consultant. You can hire other people later and move out of your home office later. For now, you need to use the KISS (Keep It Simple, Stupid) method.

3.   Take some small business courses from a local community college.

4.   Join local small business organizations.

5.   Talk to other consultants and learn from the pros.

6.   Do your homework. Read this book front to back and then do it again.

7.   Find out who your competition is and who your target market is and keep up with them.

These suggestions are not necessary to begin a consulting business, but it can help you create the most functional and viable business possible.

Home / Web-Based Consulting

Chapter 2

Research on the Consulting Industry

You can conduct some research on your own to see if wedding consulting is viable in your area. You can do a couple of different kinds of research: primary and secondary.

Primary Research

The information collected in primary research is original and collected for a specific purpose. The problem with primary research is it can be expensive and time consuming. The benefit of primary over secondary research is that it is more focused. Below are some ways you may wish to conduct your own primary research on wedding consulting.

- ♥ Telephone interviews

- ♥ Face-to-face interviews

- ♥ Internet surveys

- ♥ Mystery shopping

Telephone Interviews

These types of interviews are cheap and can focus on a specific geographic area. The interviews are structured, but they can lack depth. The advantages of telephone interviews are that they can target a geographic area — or be spread over large geographical areas — they are relatively inexpensive, and you can collect a random sampling of people. The disadvantages of telephone interviews are that often respondents hang up, the interviews are short, no visual aids can be used, and you cannot glean any information by behavior or body language.

Face-to-Face Interviews

Face-to face interviews are more intimate than other interviews. Advantages of face-to-face interviews are that they can be more in-depth, you can use pictures and other aides to assist you, and you can gather more information through behavior and body language. The disadvantages of face-to-face interviews are that they can be more costly, they can take time to arrange and conduct, and sometimes the data is not reliable because the person being interviewed wants to please the interviewer.

The Internet

The Internet is used in a number of ways to conduct surveys. These usually appear as questionnaires on Web sites, and they often offer incentives to complete the survey. Some of the advantages of Internet surveys are that they are relatively inexpensive, they can use visual aides, and people are willing to fill them out because they like the site where they located the survey. There are disadvantages of using the Internet to conduct surveys, such as not knowing how to use the software to create them, not being able to place them on wedding sites that would be the best place to use such a survey, and that some people do not like them and feel they are invasive.

Mail Survey

This may be the most common and easiest way for a wedding consultant to conduct a market survey. You can do this by purchasing a mailing list that is targeted at the market in which you wish to do research. You can buy these lists from trade associations, newspapers, or Internet list brokers. You can request lists in a specific geographical area where you wish to start your wedding consulting business. You may want to consider the following criteria when you have a company build a list for you:

1. Age

2. Gender

3. Professional women

4. Older parents

5. Divorced

6. Engaged

There are a number of different options to choose. The more superior the list you buy, the better survey results you will receive. Here are a couple of places to look at for obtaining mailing lists:

❤   **www.srds.com** — This company specializes in providing information about publications that sell their mailing lists in the Standard Rate and Data service.

❤   **www.marketingsource.com** — This company creates and sells direct mailing lists per your specifications.

❤   **www.caldwell-list.com** — This company produces custom mailing lists.

❤   **www.goleads.com** — Another company that allows you to use certain criteria to create the right mailing list.

Once you have the mailing list, you should then create a questionnaire that addresses your marketing questions and needs. Once you have completed your questionnaire, print it out on your company letterhead and make copies. If you have an e-mail list, you can just send the questionnaire via e-mail.

Buyer beware. *When you buy certain mailing lists, they may be for one use only. They will be seeded with addresses that the company can monitor. If you send out more than one mailing using the list, you could be charged for using it again.*

One way to get someone to take the survey and send it back to you through the mail is cold hard cash. If you slip a dollar bill into the envelope, a person is more likely to spend the time to fill out the survey. If you have thousands of mailings, it could become costly. This research is very important because you will use the data you gather to tailor your wedding consulting business and the services it offers. In the end, it can earn you more money in less time if you target just the right market.

Mystery Shopping

This is something you can do on your own. Call around to other wedding consultants and set up appointments. Find out what their services are and how they do business. If they charge a fee for a consultation, you need to figure that into your research budget. You can gather a lot of important information from your competition.

If you do not feel comfortable about conducting the research yourself, and you have a good-sized budget, you may consider hiring a marketing firm to do your research. They can charge between $2,000 and $8,000, depending on what type of research you want them to conduct. They do have the expertise to conduct this kind of research on your behalf, and they may have access to tools and resources that you do not. They can conduct the research, collect the data, analyze the data, and put all of the results in a report for you.

Secondary Research

This type of research is affordable. In addition, it can be done quicker than primary research. You are essentially using outside agencies and reports to conduct your research. Why reinvent the wheel when someone has already put it into existence? The drawback is that the research could have been done for purposes other than those for which you intend to use it. It can be unfocused and difficult to use for what you need. Here is a list of possible sources of secondary research.

- ♥ Trade associations

- ♥ National and local press industry magazines

- ♥ National/international governments

- ♥ Informal contacts

- ♥ Trade directories

- ♥ Published company accounts

- ♥ Business libraries

- ♥ Professional institutes and organizations

- ♥ Previously gathered marketing research

- ♥ Census data

- ♥ Public records

Here are a few Web sites that may provide the necessary information.

- ♥ **www.census.gov** — This is the United States Census Bureau site.

- ♥ **www.sba.gov** — This is the Small Business Administration site.

♥ **http://jmc.ou.edu/FredBeard/Secondary.html** — This site contains many links for sources of secondary research information.

Once you have gathered your data, you must decide how to use it. It should give you a clear idea about who your target market is. In addition, it should give you a clear idea where to best utilize your resources in advertising and marketing. You will know who your clients are, what they are looking for, and where to find them.

Often it is the understanding of the wedding consulting market — the industry and your target clientele — that is the weakest part of a wedding consultant's business plan. There is a feeling that you know all there is to know about your competitors, trends in the industry, and changes in fashion; that is, until you figure out that you do not know as much as you think you do. There is a direct correlation between the success of your business and being aware of changing trends, fashions, who your competitors are, and what your clients are looking for in their weddings. It is up to you to analyze trends, needs, and statistics. This will keep your consulting business in competition with changing markets, and you will be able to adjust your business plan quickly so that you do not lag behind.

Understanding Your Competition

Like almost any other industry, weddings and wedding planning have their own shape and structure. This shape and structure is determined by the number of competitors in the industry. In order to understand the wedding consulting industry and your competition, you must know as much as you can about the following:

♥ Competition

♥ New wedding trends and fashion

♥ Entry barriers

♥ Exit barriers

❤ Industry analysis which looks at the general industry environment in which you compete and industry trends and statistics

Competition

To understand your competition better, make a list of all of your major competitors. These can be grouped geographically or by the services they offer. After you have made your list, use the following worksheet to analyze your competition.

♡ WEDDING CONSULTING COMPETITION ANALYSIS WORKSHEET ♡

Industry Analysis Questionnaire

1. What is the number of wedding consulting businesses in your area? **Many/ Some/Few/Unknown**

2. Is the competition dominated by several large wedding consulting firms? **Yes/No/Unknown**

3. The combined market share of the three largest wedding consulting businesses is: **<40 percent/40-80 percent/>80 percent/Unknown**

4. New fashions and trends in the wedding consulting business change every: **Year/Five Years/Ten Years/Unknown**

5. The barriers that stop new competitors from entering the wedding consulting business are: **High/Medium/Low/Unknown**

6. Overall market demand in the wedding consulting industry is: **Growing/ Stable/Declining/Unknown**

7. There is a large, untapped market in the wedding consulting industry that you can find a niche in: **Yes/Maybe/No/Unknown**

8. The wedding consulting industry offers different options as far as the type of services that a wedding consultant can offer: **Extensive/Average/ Limited/Unknown**

9. Clients buy wedding consulting services based almost entirely on price: **Yes/No/Unknown**

10. Clients can use other types of services without using wedding consulting services: **Easily/With Difficulty/No/Unknown**

11. Wedding consultants in your area have a lot of influence when it comes to setting terms and prices on consulting: **Yes/No/Unknown**

♡ WEDDING CONSULTING COMPETITION ANALYSIS WORKSHEET ♡

12. Clients have a lot of bargaining power when contracting for wedding consulting services: **Yes/No/Unknown**

13. Vendors have a lot of power and play a major role in the workings of the wedding consulting industry: **Yes/No/Unknown**

14. The overall prices in the wedding consulting field have been: **Rising/ Stable/Declining/Unknown**

15. The profit margins in wedding consulting are: **Strong/Average/Weak/ Unknown**

The answers on this worksheet should give you a better understanding of the wedding consulting industry in your area and your competition. If you marked any of the answers "unknown" then you need to do further research.

New Wedding Trends and Fashion

The ever-changing trends, themes, and fashions associated with weddings are a major driver of the wedding consulting industry. How much is the changing face of weddings driving your business, and how fast is it changing? Who controls and sets the standards for modern weddings? How easily can you get information and even products associated with the new trends in modern weddings?

Entry Barriers

The barriers that prevent new competitors from setting up their own wedding consulting business are referred to as entry barriers. Some examples of these barriers may be the lack of capital, or up-front money, a small client base, geographical limitations, and ways to reach clients. There is the economy of scale to consider. This principle states that the bigger your company is, the more money you will make because larger companies can do business cheaper than small business and therefore can offer lower prices. These lower prices translate into more clients. An example of this is that a local pizza company that makes a pizza for $10.00 cannot compete with larger national chains that can make a similar pizza for $5.00. This can discourage sole proprietors from entering the wedding consulting industry.

Established businesses with a strong client base and the cost of keeping up with new wedding trends can be daunting competitors to some would-be wedding consultants.

Exit Barriers

If you decide that you do not want to continue wedding consulting there may be obstacles that could make it more difficult for you to get out; these are referred to as exit barriers. Have you invested your entire life savings and borrowed up to your eyeballs to get the business going? It may be difficult to call it quits once you have invested in the company. In addition, you may want to consider if there is any other market, such as event planning, that you could get into that would not be difficult to shift your company's focus. Knowing all that you can about the wedding consulting business can be to your advantage.

Teaming With Others

Having someone to work with can be a beneficial prospect for you both. You can share in the costs of equipment, workspace, and marketing. In addition, if the other person specializes in certain services or certain types of weddings, then the combination of the two of you can increase your client base and revenue. You can also help each other out in getting things done that one person may have difficulty doing. Depending on the type of agreement you come up with, this can also save you money, because you will not have to hire and subcontract for assistance.

There are some considerations to make when taking on a partner. If you were starting a business with just yourself as the sole owner, you would file what is called a "doing business as" (DBA). This is the process of securing the name of your business. We will explore that more in Chapter 6. For now, you must understand that if you file as a sole proprietor you are liable for losses, bankruptcy claims, legal actions, and so forth. You are personally liable for these things and so you could lose personal as well as business assets.

If you intend to have a partnership with another wedding consultant, you have a couple of options. You can form a general partnership. This is less involved than if you tried to form a corporation. Each would be responsible for what the other does, so it would not hurt to have an attorney draw up some partnership papers. They do not have to be filed legally, but it will help with possible problems and misunderstandings in the future.

If you are sure you have found the right person to form a business with, you might consider a Limited Liability Company or LLC. An LLC creates a tax structure of a partnership, but also protects the owners from personal liability. This protects an owner's personal assets.

The other type of legal arrangement that can be considered with a partner is a corporation. This goes a step beyond an LLC in that it creates a separate entity from the owners. It is an involved process that includes filing articles of corporation, electing officers, and holding an annual meeting. For most wedding consultants, this may be more trouble than it is worth. In addition, a corporation must pay corporate taxes, which can be cost prohibitive for many wedding consultants. However, there are benefits to a corporation. You can obtain financing much easier than you can alone. This can help if you want to expand or franchise your business.

If you decide to go the route of becoming a corporation, you may consider hiring an attorney. While it may save you money initially to file it yourself, it could cost you later due to complexities of corporate law.

Bridal Shows

Bridal shows are an excellent place to learn about the wedding trade, see the latest trends, and network with vendors. Every show usually has a fee to set up as a vendor, so you will need to check with the event. Try to make your application early as these events can fill up quickly.

You should have at least a fold-up table and chair to go to these events. Make sure you have plenty of business cards and brochures. Have your portfolio prominently displayed for both clients and other vendors to see. Consider making some three-sectioned folding posters to display.

Make them colorful and have pictures of the best events that you helped create. You can consider having some light classical music playing at your station. These events are usually held in large convention halls and can be rather noisy, so your music may be lost in a cacophony of sound.

You can offer brides discounts at the show if they sign up for a consultation. This does a couple of things. First, you are getting solid consultation commitments. Secondly, you can use this to determine whether setting up a booth was worth your time and effort.

You can write the event on the back of your business cards as you hand them out. When you hear from a bride later, you can ask her to let you know where she heard about your services.

In addition, have a book or pad for a mailing list. You can generate more clients after the event by using this mailing list to send out a description of your services.

You can use a few tricks to attract potential clients' attention at these events. You must realize that there are many other wedding consultants attending, so it is good to have an edge over the competition.

♥ **Offer free gifts.** Have some small items to give out to brides-to-be. These should be inexpensive and, if possible, have your information attached. These can be pens, mugs, garters, wedding planning books, coupons for other vendors, coupons for your services, and anything else you can think of.

♥ **Give out treats.** This depends on the venue. You can have a bakery make a wedding cake or two and give out pieces for people to try. While they are eating your treat, they will stay and listen to your pitch. It is a win/win situation for the bakery as you can also hand out their information.

♥ **Have a game or two set up.** You can have a garter toss, bean bag toss, or a wheel of fortune. They can win small prizes and coupons. This will get the brides to be involved, and if they have children this can definitely get them to come to your both.

❤ **Have a live musician.** Like the treats, this is a win/win proposition. If you have a harp, flute, or guitar player to perform in front of your booth, they can hand out their information as you hand out yours. People will stop and listen. Remember, they are shopping for all kinds of vendors for their wedding.

❤ **Have flowers.** Like the musician and bakery, a florist can be advertising their products while you pitch your service. Most women love to receive flowers, so when you hand them a lovely rose or carnation, you will instantly make a friend.

❤ **Remember to smile.** If you smile, other people will smile. If you make eye contact they will be more likely to come over and talk with you. Keep your conversation light and do not hit them with a heavy pitch. If they are at a bridal show, then they are shopping for services and do not need to be convinced. Your job is to make them feel at ease and comfortable with you. That initial contact and conversation is what will win you the job, not all the glitz and glamour. Brides will hire someone they trust, because handing over wedding plans to a stranger can be a very difficult and daunting task.

❤ **Always thank people** for stopping by and end with "I hope to talk to you soon." Alternatively, "I can't wait to hear more about your wedding plans." Leave them with the idea that you will see them again and that they are leaving as a friend.

Who Is My Target Audience/Main Client Source?

If you have done your marketing research correctly, you should already know some of the answers to where you will find your clients. You will know their demographics and where the greatest concentrations of your target audience are located.

With this information, you need to target your advertising and marketing efforts and budgets where they will be the most beneficial. As time passes, you will need to do more primary or secondary research to see if your target audience has shifted at all.

You will find brides frequenting the following areas and so these are the locations where your business information must be displayed:

- Churches

- Restaurants

- Florists

- Bakeries

- Wedding venues

- Music providers

- Wedding shows

- Dress shops

Anywhere they sell goods or provide services is where you need to concentrate your marketing efforts. Remember that your greatest client base will come from referrals. Remember to send out thank-you letters each time you receive a referral from a prior client. They are your greatest assets and treasures. Treat them like royalty. Without them, you do not have a viable business.

Will I Need a Lot of Money to Work From Home?

In a previous section, we learned about start-up costs. Once you have gotten past your initial investment, the cost to run a wedding consulting business is relatively low. You are providing a service, so you do not have the overhead of having to merchandise. In addition, you are working from home, so you do not have the expense of an office.

The greatest amount of money you will have to spend is on marketing, advertising, travel, and your home office expenses. These costs are minimal and should be easily absorbed by the money you will be making as a successful wedding consultant.

If you are smart with your money and keep your head on straight, you can make a lot of money with very little overhead or expenses. Remember not to allow bills to be paid late, as late fees can definitely add up and increase the expense of doing business.

Can I Work Strictly From Home?

You can work from home, but one thing you must check into is local zoning ordinances. These types of ordinances are usually in neighborhoods to reduce traffic and excessive noise that can arise by having a business next door.

Wedding consulting usually does not create excess traffic or noise, so you should not have a problem setting up shop at home. Most of your work will be in people's homes, businesses, and various wedding venues. There will not be many occasions in which a client would come to your home.

It is a good idea to check with your local government office to alleviate any questions or problems in the future. You may need a special permit. It is better to be safe and only then have all your business cards printed with your address on it.

If you do establish your business in your home, it is a good idea to have a separate area set aside for work. This will benefit you in a few ways. First, it will help you keep organized. It will be hard to keep up with your clients and the details of their weddings if the information is strewn all over your house.

Second, it will help you separate work from home. You need time away from work or it could lead to burnout. Being able to close a door allows you to end your day. In addition, if you have children, they will know that when you are in your "work" area they should not be a disturbance. If there is no defined area in the home, this can be more difficult to understand.

Third, in order to be able to deduct a home office from your taxes, you must have a separate area in your home. We will talk about the IRS and filing in Chapter 5, but for now make sure you have a defined area in your house. You can only use it for your business to use it as a tax deduction. If you use it for any personal use, you cannot claim it as a deduction.

You should consider getting a separate phone for your business. Nothing is as unprofessional as having a client call and get an answering machine that has a two-year-old stating that you are not home right now. You should have a dedicated answering machine because you will be out in the field a lot. You may have a cell phone, but this should only be used for emergencies. When you are working with a client and you are answering your cell phone every five minutes, they may not feel very important or that their time matters.

How Much Travel Is Involved?

That depends on where you live. If you live in the city and everything is close by, you will not have to travel very far. If, on the other hand, you live in the suburbs or in rural areas, then your travel will be greatly increased.

When you did your research and figured out your demographics, you were able to get an idea of where clients are located. This could mean you have to commute to get to where your brides or venues are located. Each person's situation may be different.

Even if you do not have to travel far, you will be traveling often. You will be meeting clients and vendors every day when you are in full swing. You cannot expect a florist to close their shop to show your floral arrangements; you can expect to make an appointment. This is where being organized is very important. Here are some ideas of items you may want to consider having in order to know why, when, and where you are going:

💜 **Calendar.** This has to be one of your most treasured possessions. Without it, you will be completely lost. Here are different options for a calendar.

  1. **Paper version** — This is the kind that I recommend the highest. It is low tech and so it will not run out of batteries. It is recommended that you use a pencil when using a paper calendar because you will find yourself changing appointments all of the time. Keep it close and use it often. The drawback is that if you lose it, you do not have a backup unless you create one.

  2. **Computer calendar** — Unless you intend to lug around a computer with you everywhere and have to boot it up every time you need to make or change an appointment, this may not be the best option. However, if you keep your calendar on your computer and then print a daily paper version, this can work quite nicely. You will have a backup to your work. You have to be diligent in making alterations and printing it out daily. The drawback is that it is not helpful in seeing what your appointments are on a moment's notice in the field.

  3. **PDA (Personal Digital Assistant)** — This is a small computer-like device that is mobile and gives you the ability to see your entire schedule. The drawback is that they are usually small and typing into them can be a little tricky. There are a number of different versions such as the Palm Pilot, Blackberry, and many mobile phones now double as a PDA. They are nice because they can synchronize with your computer at home as a backup. These are for

the technically inclined wedding consultants. If technology scares you, stick with the paper calendar.

♥ **Global Positioning System device (GPS).** The GPS is a radio navigation system that allows land, sea, and airborne users to determine their exact location, speed, and time 24 hours a day, in most weather conditions, anywhere in the world. GPS is used to support a broad range of military, commercial, and consumer applications. There are 24 GPS satellites (21 active, 3 spare) that are in orbit at 12,600 miles above the Earth. Each of these satellites is spaced so that from any point on earth, four satellites will be above the horizon. Each satellite contains a computer, an atomic clock, and a radio. With an understanding of its own orbit and the clock, the satellite continually broadcasts its changing position and time. On the ground, any GPS receiver contains a computer that "triangulates" its own position by getting bearings from three of the four satellites. The result is provided in the form of a geographic position — longitude and latitude — to within, for most receivers, a few meters.

Some receivers are equipped with a display screen that shows a map; the position can be shown on the map. Your receiver will be able to calculate your speed and direction of travel and give you estimated times of arrival to specified destinations. Some specialized GPS receivers can also store data for use in Geographic Information Systems (GIS) and map making.

There are a number of different sizes and models to choose from. They range in price from about $150 for hand-held models to $4,000 for car-mounted models. Some models have a color screen and some even talk to you. They can be invaluable for finding vendors, clients, and new venues. They make the days of fumbling with paper maps obsolete.

♥ **Roadside assistance insurance.** The American Automobile Association (AAA) insurance is one of these types of companies. When you are trying to get to a wedding on time, a bride does not want to hear that you have a flat tire. Make sure you are able to call for help and get it quickly. (Of course, make sure you have a spare tire in the trunk.) Make sure you have a reliable car so you make all your appointments on time. Accidents happen, and sometimes things happen that cannot be foreseen. Keeping your car well maintained and in good working order is something you do have control over. Here is a list of sites you can check out to get roadside assistance insurance:

1. **www.aaa.com** Basic membership for a year is $52. If you have ever had a flat tire or locked your keys in the car, a $1 a week charge will seem like nothing.

2. **http://www.onstar.com** If you have a General Motors car you may want to consider having On Star installed in your car. Help is only a button push away.

3. **http://www.crosscountry-auto.com/AutoClub.htm** This is another roadside assistance similar to AAA.

Look to services that are available with your cell phone. Many cell phone companies now offer roadside assistance programs for a nominal fee added to your cell phone bill. Make sure you shop and compare services offered and that you are getting the best service for your needs and budget.

If you are planning to go to trade shows and bridal showcases, then you should consider that you will be traveling sometimes long distances to get to them. Make sure you have added these shows as part of the budget.

If a bride wants a special location for her wedding, then there may be some travel involved. It could even mean a plane trip to some exotic location. Make sure you include any expenses incurred for this type of travel in your contract. These are customarily over and beyond your normal fee. You may want these expenses paid before the wedding.

Travel expenses can include tolls and parking fees. Make sure that you are keeping a good tally of your expenses. Here is a list of items you should be recording.

❤ **Mileage** — First you need to determine how many miles per gallon your vehicle is getting. Fill your gas tank full at the pump. Set your odometer to zero. The next time you fill up your tank write down how many gallons of gas you used. Take the number on your odometer and divide it by the number gallons of gas you just pumped. This will give you how many miles per gallon your car is getting. You can calculate the average cost of gas to determine how much it is costing you. Keep a record of odometer readings when you start and finish a trip. This includes going to and from a destination.

❤ Tolls

❤ Parking

❤ Car insurance

❤ Maintenance (If you keep good receipts for six months to a year, you can figure out an average cost.)

❤ Property tax

When you have been working six months to a year, you need to take these items and add them up. Divide the number by the number of months you have been recording:

$4,200/ 12 months = $350.00

In this example, $350 is the monthly travel expense you should budget. This does not even include special events or major car repair, so you may want to add another 20 percent to that number to create a buffer.

If you wish to count these expenses on your taxes, you have already created the necessary documentation that you will need. You must consider that in order to count the depreciation of your vehicle on your taxes, it must be used for a large percentage or exclusively for your work activities. Keeping good records can help prevent any questions or tax audits.

What About Liability Insurance?

The costs of covering your business and yourself from a potential lawsuit are high. It is recommended that you get liability insurance, especially if you are the sole proprietor of your wedding consulting business. If anything happens, you could lose business and personal assets. Getting liability insurance helps protect all of your assets. Even if you are an LLC, you can be sued personally in certain instances of negligence or bad business practices.

Business liability insurance will protect your wedding consulting business in the event of a lawsuit for personal injury or property damages. It will usually cover the damages from a lawsuit along with the legal costs. Depending on your business needs, there are a number of different types of liability insurance.

Types of Business Liability Insurance

General Liability Insurance: This form of business liability insurance is the most common type that wedding consultants buy. It protects your business from injury claims, property damages, and advertising claims. General liability insurance, also known as Commercial General Liability (CGL), may be the only type of business liability insurance your wedding consulting business needs.

Professional Liability Insurance: If you are providing other services in addition to wedding planning, such as marriage counseling, you will need this type of insurance. This type of liability insurance is known as errors and omissions. This coverage protects your business against malpractice, errors, negligence, and omissions. Depending on your profession, such as a licensed counselor, it may be a legal requirement to carry such a policy. Technology consultants may need this form of coverage in independent contractor work arrangements.

Product Liability Insurance: If you are offering products that you are selling or manufacturing, you should be protected in the event of a person becoming injured because of using the product. Consider the scenario of being a caterer and someone being allergic to the nuts you put in the cake. The amount of coverage and the level of risk depend on your business type. The level of risk your products pose will drive the cost of this type of coverage.

It is important to note that many venues will require liability insurance in order to use their venue for a wedding or reception. The bride and groom will need to get this insurance for their wedding. This should not go under your liability insurance. **http://www.wedsafe.com/liability. html** *is a good site to point your brides to should they need this type of insurance.*

Wedding consultants renewing an existing policy or starting a new policy need to shop for the best business liability insurance rates and coverage. Here are some tips that can help you get the best prices:

Belong to an association — There are many trade associations and business groups, such as the Chamber of Commerce, that provide members the benefit of purchasing insurance at group rates. The Association of Bridal Consultants, **http://www.bridalassn.com** is an association that offers liability insurance to its members. There are other companies offer liability insurance that can be found in wedding trade magazines.

Compare coverage — The extent of business liability coverage varies from insurer to insurer. You need to do your research and consider if and how much legal fees are covered. Review the policy details to know what is included and excluded in the coverage. Do not sign anything until you are sure that you are fully covered.

Assess wedding consultant settlements — To gain a better perspective of the amount of coverage your wedding consultant business needs, look at the wedding industry. Review the recent legal actions and settlements in the wedding planner field. Talk to peers and find their level of coverage.

Using your peer feedback and wedding industry research, determine the average legal costs and settlement to set your coverage limits.

Get the package deal — Purchasing separate types of business insurance from various insurers can quickly increase your premiums. You need to take a close look at your business needs. You may determine that it makes sense to buy a package of policies such as Business Owner's Policy (BOP) to cover your business and save on rates. Be sure to understand the extent of coverage of the package. Not every type of insurance falls under a BOP.

Find a specialist broker — Your wedding consulting business and the wedding industry has unique needs and risks. To get the best available coverage and rates, consider working with an insurance broker who knows your business and has experience in your industry.

Protecting your wedding consulting business from risks is the foundation for success. Take the necessary time to investigate your business liability insurance needs with an insurance representative, your industry association, and peers. It could be the most important decision for your consulting business's survival.

Competing Venues/Business Owners

During your market analysis, you looked up your major competitors. You may want to organize that list by your primary, secondary, and tertiary competitors. Competition is not bad. It makes your services better and helps you focus on the needs of your clients.

Having good relationships with your competitors is also a good thing. Consider all of those thousands of weddings that are occurring every weekend. One wedding consultant cannot do them all. Having a network of competitors can help everyone involved. Here is a list of reasons why:

1. There will be clients that you or your competition may not be able to get along with. If you are about to pull your hair out, you might want to call another consultant to help you out. You could either

have them take over, or ask for their help and split the fee. If they are in a bind, they may send work your way in return.

2. Due to the sheer volume of work during certain times of the year, you may find yourself in a position that you cannot possibly do four weddings in one day. Having a good relationship with another consultant can benefit both of you as you refer clients to each another.

3. Having a bad relationship with a competitor really does not have any advantages. You spend more of your valuable time trying to undermine your competition instead of concentrating on improving your business.

4. Having a good relationship with your competition can help you set reasonable prices. If a client is finding that all of the wedding consultants in the area have about the same price, then they will look for the best fit according to what they want out of their wedding rather than who is the cheapest. In addition, your competitors are less likely to try to undercut your price if you have a good working relationship with them.

5. You can focus on certain aspects of weddings and you can specialize. If you know what your competition is doing and you agree that you are going to try to work in a different niche, then you can specialize in the type of weddings you want to. In addition, you can refer potential clients to someone else if you do not feel you can offer them what they want.

In certain areas, this may be a real Pollyanna way of looking at things. In markets that are flooded with wedding consultants and competition, you may not get your competitors to have a civil business relationship with you. In that case, keep a close eye on what they are doing as far as their prices and the way they do business. You can learn a lot. Try to adjust your prices as needed to keep your head above water, because price does matter when there are huge gaps.

One of the best ways to see what your competition is doing is to visit their booths during wedding shows and invite them to do the same. If you are lucky enough to have a wedding consultant organization near where you live and work, it is well worth joining, for no better reason than to meet and know your competitors.

Always keep an open mind. You can always learn something new from what others are doing. Your competitor may have just returned from a fashion show in New York and is offering New York–style weddings. You can learn what the new trends and fashions are and try to incorporate them into your business. If you do not stay on top, you will lose out. If price were no object for brides, they would choose the best wedding possible led by the most current and knowledgeable wedding consultant around, so you should offer them the best.

The other things to consider are vendors and venues. You want to try to secure your territory by using particular venues for weddings. In addition, you want a variety of places to choose from because not every bride wants the same thing. Your competitors will be competing for the same venues on the same dates. Try to work out compromises. If you have a good relationship with your competitor, you are more likely to work out a compromise.

It is the same situation with vendors. There may be a limited number of vendors in your area. You need to have good relationships with them because your competition is trying to do the same. If a vendor likes you and you have a good relationship with them, you are more likely to get better deals than they offer your competition. This means more money in your pocket, which allows you to offer more competitive wedding packages.

Since there is a finite number of vendors, find your own niche so that you will not have to compete for dates that a vendor is available to serve you.

Learning How to Work Independently

In the first chapter, there was a list of different traits that made a successful wedding consultant. The ability to work independently was one of them. If you have to be told what to do, you will fall behind and not be able to keep up with deadlines and schedules. There will be times that unexpected events happen. Suppose there is a forecast for rain, and your bride had decided on an outdoor wedding. You must be the one to have an alternate plan and be ready to insist that the bride change the venue so that the entire wedding is not a wash-out. Being independent is essential. You cannot wait for the bride to tell you that she thinks it is going to rain and it is an hour before the wedding. She hired you because she wanted you to take care of all the details. If the couple had the time to tell everyone what to do at every point in the process, they would not need a wedding consultant.

In addition to thinking ahead and making plans on your own, you must be firm in your decisions. If you waver and are not sure about your decisions, the family will lose their confidence in you. This will not only affect you during this wedding, but will hurt your word-of-mouth advertising later.

You must learn the word "NO." It only has two letters, but it is a very powerful word. Good leaders and organizers know that using the word "no" is essential. Not only must you be able to say the word, you must stand by it. Even if later you think you made a mistake, that is fine, but in order for others to respect your decisions you must stand by them. That does not mean you have to be insulting, because that could get you fired. What it does mean is that if someone challenges you, you must be able to back your decision.

Let us say for instance that a bride wants to invite 300 people to a wedding at a venue that will only hold 150, you must be able to tell the bride, "No, that will not work." The bride may argue with you that they have 300 best friends and that they all have to be invited; you must stick by your answer. You can go on to explain that even if you got more chairs that the fire marshal will not allow it. You can remind the bride that she hired you for your expertise and knowledge. You can offer to cut down the list or change the venue.

If, on the other hand, you bow to the wishes of the bride and say, "Well, I will see what I can do. Maybe they will let people stand in the back." This may seem to be a reasonable reply, but it can lead to disaster and mistrust later. When you return to the bride with the answer that you already knew was going to be the likely answer, she may become angry and feel that you misled her. A worst-case scenario is that she may have already sent out the invitations to 300 people. So being able to be independent and stick by your decisions is very important. It builds self-confidence and trust with your clients.

A Business Plan: What Is It & Do I Need One?

Chapter 3

I t takes more than just motivation and talent to have a successful wedding consulting business. It also takes research and planning. Small mistakes in the beginning do not spell disaster; however, it can be difficult to get back on track and regain the advantage. If you take the needed time in the beginning to explore and evaluate your business and personal goals, you can then use what information you gain to create a comprehensive and successful business plan that can help you achieve your goals more easily.

Developing a great business plan can force you to process and work through important issues that ordinarily you may not have considered.

The final plan you develop will then become a powerful tool as you begin your wedding consulting business.

The purpose of a business plan is to assist you in creating a roadmap that you will need to help you reach your business goals. In addition, a business plan also provides you a way to track and see your progress as you begin and grow your consulting business.

When you set out on a trip, you usually begin it by hopping in a car and driving. First, you need a destination. Then you need a road map to reach your destination. A successful and profitable wedding consulting business is your destination. Your business plan then becomes the road map to reach that destination. A business plan will keep you focused on your journey.

It will show you where you are and how far you still need to go. If it is detailed and well thought out, it can also show you the obstacles ahead and ways around them.

Many moneylenders require a complete business plan before they will lend you money. It provides the lender a look at the details of your business and more importantly if you have included a way to pay them back. They want to know that your business is a viable one, and that you are a safe investment. If you have gaps or do not take the time necessary to create an outstanding business plan, they may not take the risk of lending the money you need to begin your venture. Here is a rundown of what a good business plan will do and why you need it:

- A business plan is an examination of your service (wedding consulting).

- It shows what the market is and who your target audience is. You already began this process in Chapter 1.

- It lists your competitors. You created this list in Chapter 2.

- It will show your plan for marketing and sales. You will explore this more in Chapter 7.

- It will list the costs of production. You also began this list in Chapter 1.

- If you will have other people working with or under you, your business plan with contain a management plan.

- You will list your finances. You have already begun the process of figuring out what things will cost and what your debt is like. You will learn about this through this chapter.

- Your business plan must outline each and every activity in detail, and will include timing and constraints.

You will learn about each section of the business plan. Contained at the end of this book in the appendix and on the CD-ROM is a sample Business Plan and a Business Plan Template you can use.

Executive Summary

This section of your business plan may be the smallest section. Do not underestimate its importance. It will summarize who you are, what your company does, where your company is going, and how you are going to get there. When you are trying to secure finances, you may have just a couple of minutes to grab their attention. That is why this summary is so important. If it is not eye-catching and does not contain the necessary information, the investor may not read any further.

Your executive summary must be as thorough as possible while being compelling, enticing the reader to continue. This summary must do the following:

- Describe your company

- Describe what wedding consulting is and, more importantly, what your wedding consulting business offers

- Describe market opportunities

All of this must be done in a concise and engaging manner.

Even though your executive summary will appear in the beginning of your business plan, you should create it last. You should write at least a paragraph to describe each section of your business plan. You should also end your executive summary with a listing of the amount of money required. Make sure that you list major advantages your company will have over the competition. One final item your summary should contain is a note that you have additional backup information.

A well-conceived and complete business plan will let the reader get a quick snapshot of your business, your plans, and what you will need to make it all happen. You should include all of your goals and hopes for your wedding consulting business. Your executive summary will capture all of the important parts of your plan. Try not to make your summary too long or detailed. Remember, it is a just a quick snapshot of the rest of the document. It is meant to grab the reader's attention and leave them wanting to read further. As a rule of thumb, it should be no longer than two pages.

Objectives

In this section, you will list all the major goals you have set for your wedding consulting business. It should include the objectives you want to meet to achieve your goals.

Mission

The mission statement will be a statement of your company's mission or purpose. The statement goes further to answer the question of where you want to go and what you want your company to become. Be sure that your mission includes the products or services your wedding consulting business will be offering. You should describe where you want your company to be in three to five years.

Keys to Success

In this area will be contained your values statements. This is the set of beliefs and principles that guide your wedding consulting company's actions and decisions.

Company Summary

The company summary describes the purpose of your business, using your mission statement and your keys to success. The company summary will identify your company's specific capabilities and resources. You can include a brief description of everything you bring to the wedding industry that is unique. This will include your management team, company organization, products and services, company operations, and marketing potential. This is a summary and you will go into detail in the areas in later sections.

Company Ownership

This section is simply who the owners are and what type of company it is. It can even state what the plans for ownership are in the future.

Start-Up Summary

The start-up summary should include key financial documents to support your projections. It is important that your financials and your narrative mirror each other and work together. If these two parts do not match, it will send a big red flag to any potential investors. You are saying to your investors that you are either too optimistic about your sales, or you do not understand the numbers. If you send this chaotic message, you could potentially lose an investor's interest. Spend the time and effort to create and describe your financial projections by using several standard financial statements. Once you have the numbers, back it up with your narrative. It is understandable to any investor that these are merely estimates. What it does is provide them with a glimpse of where you stand today and where you expect to be in the near and distant future.

Company Locations and Facilities

This section reviews your business location and operations. You will state whether you are a home-based business or have an office. You will discuss where your target clientele is and where you plan to work most of the time.

Services

This section describes the particular services that your wedding consultation company will offer. Be as detailed and comprehensive as possible. Mention why your services are unique and better than the competition's.

In this section, make sure you include the following:

1. Describe your services. If you offer more than one service, outline each service in detail.

2. What does your wedding planning service deliver?

3. What is the primary application of your service? What is the secondary application?

4. What need does your service fill?

5. Who are your customers?

6. What are the customer benefits?

7. What makes your service different?

8. Emphasize the uniqueness of your services.

9. State advantages and disadvantages of your services.

10. State strengths and weaknesses of your services.

11. Why will a customer buy your particular service?

12. Do you have any patents, trademarks, or copyrights associated with your business?

13. What stage of development are you in with your wedding consulting service?

14. What is the price sensitivity associated with your services?

15. What is your unique selling point?

16. What is your wedding service's life cycle?

Market Analysis Summary

In this section, you will be discussing the analysis provided by determining and defining the characteristics of the market you will be targeting for sales and the measurement of the wedding market's capacity to buy your services. This analysis will identify and quantify the customers you will be targeting for sales. You will need to understand both the strength and size of the market in which you will be competing. The analysis of your competition will help you better formulate and shape your plans. In previous chapters, you have learned about identifying your market. In this section of your business plan you will need to define and describe the overall market in which you will be competing. In Chapter 2, you defined your market through different forms of market research. You should include your findings in this section. In your analysis, you will refer to these numbers, and be prepared to explain how you reached each assumption in your marketing analysis. Be sure you can verify every finding that you have contained in your market analysis summary. This verification will come from articles in magazines, trade publications, newspapers, book references, research data, and customer surveys. If you had an outside agency do your analysis, be sure to refer to the report and attach it to your business plan.

To assist you in your market analysis you can use the following worksheet:

MARKET ANALYSIS	1ST LEVEL	2ND LEVEL	3RD LEVEL
What is the total size of your targeted wedding market? Each region will be broken down into 1st, 2nd, and 3rd.			
Local			
Regional			
What are historical, current, and future (assumed) growth rates of the wedding industry?			
Historical			
Current			
What changing needs do you see in the future use of wedding consulting?			

MARKET ANALYSIS	1ST LEVEL	2ND LEVEL	3RD LEVEL
Are there any wedding industry studies or statistics that you can source?			
Describe any recent wedding industry and wedding consulting industry developments.			
List any identifiable market niches for wedding consulting.			
What are or will be your customers' needs and desires for their wedding and your service?			
Are there any common attributes that your clients in your identified market have in common?			
What is your plan for attracting and finding clients?			
What kind of advertising is your target market responsive to?			
What do existing customers like about your wedding consulting service?			
Who else has a need for the service you supply?			
Will you be offering the type of service that couples planning to wed will buy?			
Are your target markets clients, businesses, or both?			

Market Segmentation

This section of the business plan will describe the subset of prospects that are most likely to purchase your service. If done properly, this section will help to ensure the highest return for your marketing and sales expenditures. Depending on whether you are selling your services to individual consumers or to particular businesses such as specific venues, there are definite differences in what you will consider when defining market segments.

We will assume that your market is local or regional. Let us suppose that you reside in a community of about 25,000 people. You will need to figure out the demographics of your particular community. Then you will break them up into segments. Here is a sample:

- Age: 20s, 30s, 40s, 50s, elderly

- Gender: male, female

- Education: high school, bachelor's degree, postgraduate degree

- Income: low, middle, high

- Marital status: single, married, engaged

- Ethnic background

- Religious background

You can locate this information through the newspaper, local town hall, library, or Chamber of Commerce.

You will then break up and segment the market using psychographics:

Psychographics are attributes relating to personality, values, attitudes, interests, or lifestyles. These are also referred to as IAO variables (for Interests, Attitudes, and Opinions).

- Social class: low, middle, high

- Lifestyle: conservative, trendy, risk taking, sporty

- Interests: sports, shopping, reading, movies

- Attitudes: environmentally minded, conservationist

You may want to figure out their buying patterns: they may buy locally, in bulk, on sale, or seasonally. You might want to figure out who makes the decisions on buying. You should have a good idea who your target client will be. You could even include a description of your target client.

"Middle-class woman, 27 to 29 years old. She is looking for a bargain and will be the decision maker when it comes to wedding planning."

If you are on the ball, you might even know the current number of eligible women that could use your service and live in your area. Knowing this number can direct your marketing and let your investors know how much potential revenue you can expect.

There may be a number of brides that do not know about your wedding consulting business. Each of these brides is a potential client. Sometimes they have heard about your service but do not know the difference between your wedding consulting business and other companies offering similar services. This means that you have your job cut out for you. You have to target this group in order to let them know who you are and why they cannot live without you.

For example, if you want to extend your target group to women ages 21 to 32, then you must find ways to target this age group and create a bigger, more profitable market for you to capture.

You may also find in your research that your target audience is too small and that, out of a population of 25,000, only 100 people fall into your target age of 27 to 29 years old. If these 100 people are rich and will pay any price for your service then you have nothing to fear. If, on the other hand, they are lower- or middle-class women, then you may have to start your process over again. You may want to widen your market and redefine the services you will offer as a wedding consultant or where you plan to offer your services.

Market Analysis

This pie chart breaks down your market segments and creates a visual representation. Some investors like to see what you are talking about. You have to balance the number of charts and graphs in your business plan, but the right amount can look professional and can be just the edge you need.

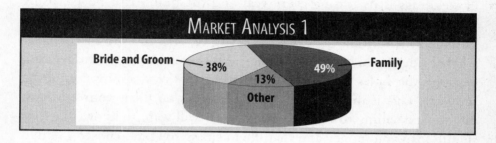

MARKET ANALYSIS 2		2003	2004	2005	2006	2007	
Potential Customers	Growth						CAGR
Brides & Grooms	5.0%	1,500	1,575	1,654	1,737	1,824	5.01%
Family Members	5.0%	5,000	5,250	5,513	5,789	6,078	5.00%
Other	5.0%	1,000	1,050	1,103	1,158	1,216	5.01%
Total	5.0%	7,500	7,875	8,270	8,684	9,118	5.00%

* CAGR - Compound Annual growth Rate is the year-over-year growth rate for an investment over a specified period of time. The compound annual growth rate is calculated by taking the nth roote of the total percentage growth rate, where n is the number of years in the period being considered.

$$CAGR = \left(\frac{Ending\ Value}{Beginning\ Value} \right)^{(1\ +\ \#\ of\ years)} -1$$

Target Market Segment Strategy

In this section, you will write out what your strategy will be for accessing your target audience. These can be items such as wedding and bridal shows, or placing flyers and business cards in places where brides are likely to see them, such as florists, venues, and caterers. Once you gain the attention of the target market, you will write out your plan for securing their business and future business prospects. Ideas in this section can be competitive prices, offering themed weddings, and special packages.

Market Needs

The wedding industry has a need for more consultants as the number of weddings is increasing every year and the number of people using wedding consultants is on the rise. This creates a niche in the industry. Finding a niche in the market is the key to success. You will also describe why a bride would choose to use a wedding consultant. In this section, describe the holes that need to be filled in the wedding consulting industry. This is important not only to help you focus your business, but anyone willing to finance your venture will want to know why they should loan you money and that the business you have chosen to build will be successful.

Service Business Analysis

In this section, you should consider how your business is a cut above the rest. What services will you offer that will attract brides? Analyze each item or service point by point. This can be an important exercise to sculpt your business into something unique.

Competition and Buying Patterns

In this section, you will analyze your competition. Who are they? Where are they? What do they offer? Try to be as thorough as possible. This list will be important to you in years to come as it will be added to and edited. It is something that a person looking at your business plan will want to study. Having a good idea of who your competition is and what they have to offer can help you decide whether the marketing area is flooded with wedding consultants or is lacking. Keeping an up-to-date list of competitors gives you the edge of knowing if your services and prices are competitive enough to keep your company afloat. Look at the Web sites and the materials that your competition offers and study them closely. Does it provide you with numbers of clients? Does it provide you with the cost of their services? What seems to be their target market?

Strategy and Implementation Summary

This section will contain your marketing strategy and how you plan to implement it. Will you have a Web site? Will you have a professional logo created? What kind of business and marketing materials will you have printed and created? How will you distribute these so they get to your target market? This is just a summary and should be clear and to the point.

Competitive Edge

What gives your company the competitive edge over the competition? Is it your experience? Is it your relationship with local vendors and venues? Is it your education? It can be something as simple as your easygoing personality or your trendy attire. This needs to be a list of the things that your competition wishes they had.

Sales Strategy

Where do you plan to advertise your business? Will it be in the papers, magazines, Internet ads, or another Web site? How much will this cost? The next step is to calculate how much sales you have in a year. If you follow some of the suggestions in this book concerning giving business cards and conducting surveys you will have a clearer understanding how your advertising is affecting your sales. You can make some forecasts on the number of sales based upon your past performance. This helps you to create a budget and know when to put your advertising into high gear should your projections begin to slip. You can also track whom exactly you are selling your services to the most. Is it the bride, groom, or family? This helps you direct your marketing to the group you are selling to the most.

There will be more components to your business plan described later in the book. The components listed above are ones that are recommended to begin your business with. As you grow, add employees, and review your business's progress and viability, you will be adding sections, information, and data to your business plan.

SALES FORECAST			
	2007	2008	2009
Brides & Grooms	$54,200	$65,040	$71,544
Family Members	$25,800	$30,960	$34,056
Other	$15,300	$18,360	$20,196
Total Sales	$95,300	$114,360	$125,796
Other	$0	$0	$0

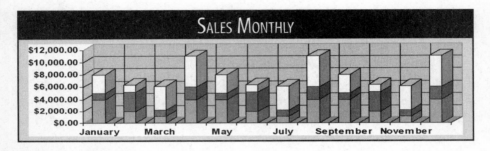

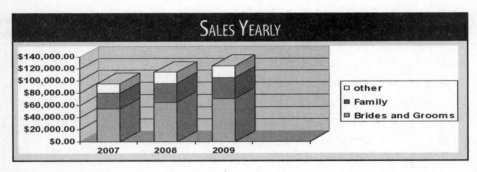

The Top Seven Suggestions for New Wedding Consultants

1. **You have to be willing to be open to suggestions.**

2. **You must be willing to create a viable business.** Sometimes new consultants have many outside-the-box ideas about the way the business should be. You need to be willing to create a wedding consultant business that follows some conventional rules so that

you can be successful. As you grow, you can become more creative and trend setting.

3. **Do not try to reinvent the wheel.** The wedding consulting business is a viable business already. Make sure your marketing plan works and that you are creating a business that will have real potential to succeed and grow. Do not delude yourself and ignore your market analysis.

4. **Be open and give your clients the opportunity to give you feedback.** A simple survey at the end is very helpful. This is truly the way to make your business grow, by listening to your clients' wants and needs, rather than imposing what you believe they want and need. If your clients feel that they are being heard, it will raise their opinion of your service and this will translate to a greater number of future sales.

5. **Use your business plan.** If you spend a lot of time creating and writing it, do not just put it in a drawer somewhere when you are done. Believe in it and use it. Successful wedding consultants follow and alter their plan as they go. It helps keep you on track and focus on finances and how you planned to do business.

6. **Stick with your resolve.** Even if you may end up being wrong, see it through. If you need to make changes along the way, that is fine, but do not be afraid of mistakes — they help you to learn.

7. **Do not be stubborn.** Ask for help when you need it. You may be a solo act when it comes to actual wedding consulting, but you may need others to help you along the way. Your business plan is the best way to communicate with others where you need help. It is the blueprint of your operations. With this operations manual other professionals can quickly assess and help you when you need help and make suggestions about how to make things run smoother and more efficiently.

Writing a great business plan can be a difficult task. Here is a list of suggestions that can make the task a little easier to manage:

1. **Do not try to complete the entire plan all at once.** Do it in small sessions and try to write a little bit at a time. Once you have some ideas written down, find someone that can read objectively and get their honest opinion and guidance. This does not have to be a businessperson and, in some situations, it may be better if they are not. They can give a fresh, unbiased opinion that may prove to be helpful in your quest to write the best plan possible.

2. **Let all your ideas flow naturally.** Do not worry about the format until you are ready to put it in the final draft. Being too concerned with format can take away from the creative process. You must be able to capture the essence and passion of your wedding consultant business while including all of the financial and technical pieces as well.

3. **You must have accurate financial components and you have to make the numbers work.** It is a fine balancing act. You must move them with your passion and your financial sense in order to get financial backers.

4. **Remember, you are not writing a book.** You want to include charts, tables, and graphs to present and analyze information. Visual presentation of your numbers can really grab someone's attention, and it can help them understand the facts and figures you are presenting.

5. **It is essential that you include certain key components in your business plan.** In your goals and mission statement section, make sure that you are developing realistic strategies to meet those goals. You are giving a vision of the way your business is now and what you project your business will be like in the future.

♥ Something to consider adding to your mission statement to make it stand out is why you have chosen to create your wedding consulting business. Your vision and values statements should be clear, concise, and right to the point.

♥ Your goals statement should capture what you plan to do with your business and how you plan to achieve it. The goals that you create are clearer when they are time based and measurable. The most important aspect of your goals is that they are not pie-in-the-sky ideas. They must be achievable, and you must have the numbers and research to support it.

♥ Be clear when you lay out your strategies that you intend to use to achieve your goals. They should also include who will be responsible for achieving the goals you have created. Your strategies may include more than one goal, or one goal may have a number of strategies.

6. **If you plan to have a partnership or create a company then you may want to consider using a well-connected team.** You may have heard the adage it is not what you know, but whom you know. If investors know people that you are working with or know people that are on your board, you have a better chance in securing financial backing for your wedding consulting business. If you are a sole proprietor, you may want to get letters of support and recommendation from people to help you on your way.

7. **Keep your press.** If there is anything in media form, such as newspaper or magazines, about you or your business be sure to save them. It is a good idea to get some public relations started, such as publishing an article or doing an interview in a wedding industry media venue, or even local media outlets.

8. **Keep your plan professional.** Stick to the facts and always base your statements on the facts you present. Do not use generalizations

or statements such as, "My business will be a grand success." Investors want to hear about numbers and facts. They will create their own opinions about the potential of your wedding consulting business on their own.

9. **In addition to keeping your plan fact based, keep it lean.** Do not try to fluff it up with too much detail. Make it clear, concise, and straight to the point. If you create the next great American novel out of it, people will only skim it and will not be very interested in your plan. If it is interesting and a quick read, you are more likely to get a positive response.

10. **Involve others in the process of your business plan,** especially if you have others working with you or business partners, or even vendors that you will be working exclusively with. Also include what they have to offer and what they will be adding to your business. Have your key people involved in the process. Not only will it create a better plan, but it can work out other business-related concerns as well. If you have everyone involved, they will have more buy-in into the business and its goals.

11. **Make sure that you are reviewing your plan at least annually, if not more often.** This is not just a review of the budget and finances. You should review your goal and vision statement to see if it still fits. In addition, as your business grows you need to make sure that your business plan and the goals of the company grow with it. If you only review the numbers, you may miss the opportunity to grow and flourish, even as a sole proprietor. You need to review where you have been, where you are, and where you intend to go. This will keep you on track and grant you abundance and success. Wedding consulting businesses that only focus on the budget and numbers often fail to stay in business over the long term.

12. **Your business plan can be a powerful tool.** It can help you improve your overall job and business performance. If you have partners or vendors that you regularly work with, try to meet with them about

once a month. Review how the business plan is going and how the consulting business's performance is. Review the numbers and see if you are continuing to stay within your projected budget and review any new competition that may have arisen.

13. **If you are lucky enough to find one, look for a mentor.** This would be someone that has experience in small business or the wedding industry that believes in you and your company. They can offer you advice and support when needed to make sound business decisions, help you with your business plan, and be there when your wedding consulting business has its inevitable difficulties.

14. **Do you live near a university?** Does it have a Master's of Business Administration (MBA) program? This may present a unique opportunity for you. Many MBA students must create a complete and concise business plan as part of their program. You can send your business plan to be reviewed by an MBA and get suggestions on how to improve it. This professional help is free and the students are motivated to get it right.

15. **Make friends with vendors and other small business owners.** You can join a Chamber of Commerce or a similar business group. Do not be afraid to ask other people questions. In addition, you can offer suggestions to help other businesses by offering your services as a wedding consultant. You suggest that they can help you in your business with their knowledge and area of expertise.

16. **Try to locate a university-affiliated Small Business Development Center.** These are great resources as they often offer free advice and free or inexpensive workshops to small business owners like you. They provide resources and information regarding every aspect of business. You can find such services as one-day seminars on getting your business started, free one-on-one counseling, clinics on the legal aspects of your business, online resources, and downloadable forms.

EXECUTIVE SUMMARY WORKSHEET

Business Plan of _____ (name of your wedding consulting business)

The purpose of the company is to provide wedding consulting services. (If you want to list the particular services that your business will offer, list them here.) ___
_____

The mission statement of (company name) is as follows:_____
_____

The long-term goals of (company name) are to_____
_____

Market Analysis

The annual gross sales of the wedding consulting industry are approximately
$ _____.

Service Analysis

The service that (company name) will provide is wedding consulting (you can be more specific if you wish)_____

(Company name) is unique in the wedding consulting industry because _____
_____

Business Operations

The (company name) will be operated by (names of the owners)_____
_____

Management of the Company

The company will be managed by _____(This can be different than the owners in certain situations)

The desired qualifications of the key management personnel are _____
_____(Fill this in if you have other people working with you. You can ignore it if you have sole proprietorship.)

Market Strategy

The target market for this service is _____

The marketing plan for (company name) is _____

Financial Plans

(Company name) annual revenue projections are _____

(Company name) immediate and long-term financing needs are _____
_____

Initial Start-Up Costs

Wedding consulting is one of those rare businesses that eager entrepreneurs can jump into, backed by just a modest amount of capital, a vision, and lots of positive enthusiasm.

The reason wedding consulting is so easy to begin is that it is a home-based business; therefore, the start-up costs are usually minimal. Wedding consultants who are working out of their home do not have the normal overhead associated with renting an office space. In addition, a wedding consultant may already own the office equipment needed to begin a home-based business. This further reduces the up-front costs.

For instance, wedding consultants can use their dining room table as a desk, their home phone, and their own personal computer with a printer attached.

There is no product, so you do not have any inventory to purchase. At least initially, you will not have products. As your business grows, you may want to own wedding props and merchandise. This can add to your income, as you do not need to go to an outside source every time and rent it. Initially, these items are not necessary to own.

For some jobs, you need a special wardrobe or uniform. As a wedding consultant, one or two wedding outfits that are modest are probably all you need. These can be used for weddings or business meetings. A wedding consultant may already have these outfits in his or her closet. Other than that, jeans and a T-shirt will work, as you may be doing some manual labor like setting up a party. You do not even have to invest much in your wardrobe.

Operations

In addition to supplies, there will be some operations costs. This is true whether you are working out of your home or have a separate office. There are phone bills, gas, and Internet costs. In addition, there is the cost of your time. You need to start thinking about how much you are worth per hour.

There are day-to-day administrative activities that have to be done. When you are starting out, you will be spending a lot of time on the phone, which does not generate money but needs to be done. You have to figure that this time will pay off as you begin to get jobs. That is why it is important that you have money saved for operation costs for the first few months until your business begins to get off the ground.

In addition to calling potential clients, you will be calling vendors. You have to spend the time to develop relationships with these vendors. In addition, you will want to start making lists of what they have to offer and at what price. As your consulting business grows, you may employ contract or temporary help during weddings. You will need to spend time meeting with them on a regular basis to provide instructions and go over details. As you begin to get clients, you will have to spend a significant amount of time with them. This includes meetings and updates as well as accompanying them to meetings with vendors, hairstylists, and florists.

That is just the fun stuff. You then have to spend time doing paperwork. If you do not discipline yourself to spend time every day doing some paperwork, you will fall behind and become disorganized. This will affect the way you do business and can affect whether or not you are able to get future clients. Part of the paperwork will be contracts to review, tax forms to file, and other business-related papers that will need attending to.

It is important that you keep clear records of the choices your brides make, the status of wedding day plans, and other important details. You need to write everything down and keep a good accounting of it. Do not rely on your memory alone. The sheer number of details that you will have to keep up with for each wedding can be overwhelming. The more organized you are, the better off you will be.

All of these day-to-day procedures need to be considered when figuring out your fee because none of these activities is what is going to pay your bills. It is the actual doing the wedding planning, not the paperwork, that will keep the lights on. Consider that at least 20 to 30 percent of your time will be taken up with the day-to-day operations.

One of the initial costs involved in becoming a wedding consultant is office supplies. If you have a home-based business, these initial costs should be minimal. Under the section "Comparison of Brick-and-Mortar versus Home-Based," we will look at a more itemized list of supplies. If you have a phone, a pad of paper, and a pen, you are ready to go. Although having some basic supplies will make your job a lot easier.

Consultations

You will have to consider whether you will charge for consultations. There are consultants that do initial consultations free of charge. Again, you must decide how much money your time is worth. If you want to give away your time for free, that is a choice you will have to make. Charging a fee will not lose you business, however.

Consultations are a time to determine what a bride wants and how much she wants to turn over to you. These generally take up to an hour to complete and a fee of about $50 an hour is reasonable. Remember that you are a professional. Doctors and lawyers charge consultation fees and so should you.

Research shows that the fee for a single consultation typically ranges from $175 in smaller communities to as much as $500 in metropolitan areas. You can offer to cut or return your fee should the bride decide to hire you as a wedding consultant.

A fee also helps focus your time. Some brides are not serious about hiring a consultant and may just be shopping around. Charging a fee will discourage these types of brides taking up an hour of your time.

The Wedding Day

There may be other small or hidden fees you will also need to consider. Some wedding consultants supply special extras for their clients. It can be as simple as snacks before the wedding for the wedding party or taking a special picture and putting it in a frame for the couple. These extras are not usually part of the package, but they can win you points for positive word of mouth, which is worth more than gold.

A consultant may subcontract extra help on the wedding day to act as greeters, runners, or to help set up the area. The consultant rather than the bride hires these, so the consultant must figure this cost into their budget for a wedding. These contract workers can be paid by the hour or by the event. In either case, this extra fee must be factored in when setting fees for packages that are offered by the wedding consultant. The consultant cannot afford to absorb every small hidden fee or they will go broke. This must be added upfront in the fees that will be charged by the consultant. They do not have to be a line item on a contract, but the consultant must figure it into their own budget.

Mistakes to Avoid

1.   Act, do not react. If you are proactive and have a plan ahead of time, you will save yourself time and money later. You can do this by being conscious of your competition, how the market changes, and new opportunities to find and secure clients.

2.   Never underestimate the amount of finances it takes to start a wedding consulting business. If you spend the time and effort to complete a viable business plan you should be well aware of how much it will cost and what your prospects are. If you underestimate or do not calculate correctly, you could end up out of business before you know it.

3.   In addition to finances, you should not underestimate the amount of time you need to commit to creating the best wedding consulting business possible. You will need to make sure you calculate traveling time, marketing, and searching for new clients. This time will be the greatest when you begin your business. It may taper off in a year or two. Do not make a mistake and think that wedding

consulting is a nine-to-five job that you can squeeze into a four- to five-workday week. Remember that most weddings take place on the weekend when people are available, and so your weekend time will be at a premium. You can find yourself overwhelmed quickly if you do not commit the time necessary and keep up with your schedule.

4. Do not try to do everything yourself. Use professionals that can help you with the business end of your consulting business. You can do some things on your own by reading books and finding sources online. The legal and financial suggestions and tools in this books are a great resource, but if you have the chance to speak with an attorney or accountant, they can help you. Do not turn down the opportunity if it arises, or if you have some extra money in your budget to hire one. They can help you put your best foot forward and answer legal and tax questions that you may not find here. You must realize that taxes change constantly and what may have been valid a year ago may not be now.

5. If there are retired consultants or other legal professionals available, take advantage. If they were successful, they can be a fount of wonderful and useful information. They can help you avoid the mistakes they made. Listen, take notes, and learn.

Strategies for Successful Consulting

While wedding consulting can be a very rewarding business, it can also be a very stressful one. There is competition out there, and it can be cutthroat. In order to be successful, you need to keep your edge and always be striving to improve your skills and the way you do business. If you are stuck in a rut, it can adversely affect your client base as new consultants come on the scene with fresh ideas and have a greater knowledge of current trends in the wedding industry.

1. Create a portfolio of satisfied clients. The greatest asset that a wedding consultant has is positive word-of-mouth advertising. In

the wedding business, reputation is everything. Having a portfolio of your accomplishments and positive affirmations from former clients can help you to convince future clients of your worth. Build an album of pictures and letters, and organize it by wedding. Have it set up so that you can show the client your work from start to finish. It is important that you collect pictures and get a recommendation from a bride before you conclude your business with her. Be sure to send a thank-you note to the newlyweds with a couple of business cards included.

2.   Be current on wedding trends and etiquette. A good way to do this is to read bridal magazines and other fashion magazines. Learn about floral arranging and decorations — what is in and what is yesterday. Look around bridal shops and attend bridal shows to see what the latest trends are in wedding attire. If you have the time, try to attend other weddings. You can glean a lot of information and generate ideas for use in your business. In addition, you can learn from others' mistakes and disasters in order to avoid the same pitfalls. Make sure you write down your ideas. Always keep a small notebook handy. Do not rely on your memory. Another good idea is to always carry a camera and never forget to carry your business cards.

3.   Develop and review your vendor network. You need to make sure you have current names and addresses of vendors. Always be on the lookout for new vendors as they may offer you new services, better services, and better prices. Establish a network of reliable suppliers. Make sure you develop positive, lasting relationships with your vendors. They are your lifeblood. Take them out to lunch, send them cards during the holidays, and try to remember their birthdays. These little details can pay off big in the end. They can often steer work your way. If you have bad relationships, the opposite could be true and it can put you out of business. As you develop good relationships, you can offer better prices on goods and services. You can extend the savings to your clients, or it can increase your profits.

4.   Work on your people skills. Wedding coordination is a people-centered business. Your survival often depends on how well you work with your clients. Brides, grooms, and families can get stressed out during a wedding. The ability to handle stressful situations and provide support and understanding can divert a wedding disaster. People will not forget your people skills, and this again translates to word-of-mouth advertising for future jobs. You can keep your skills sharp by attending business seminars or take business or communication classes at a local community college. You have to keep a cool head under the greatest times of stress. Take time for yourself and make sure you plan breaks in your year. If you are burned out then your level of tolerance and ability to successfully deal with families will decrease. This can have an adverse affect on your business.

The Wedding Industry and You

You should get to know the industry. You can do this by visiting wedding sites, reading wedding magazines, joining wedding consulting organizations, and attending bridal fairs as a guest rather than a participant. If you attend a fair as a participant you may not have much time to see what other people are doing, meet vendors, and really see what is out there. When you are a participant, you are standing at a table waiting for people to come to you.

The wedding industry is large and knowing about it both locally and nationally has its advantages. As changes in trends and business practices occur you will be informed and able to adjust your business accordingly.

Having subscriptions to wedding magazines not only gives you an idea of what is going on in the wedding industry, but it is also a tool you can use with brides to help generate ideas about jewelry, décor, and flowers. It can help refine ideas that are in a bride's head but she is having difficulty communicating. Having various magazines can help her point at a particular dress and say, "That's it." It also gives you an idea of what things are going to cost and what you need to be charging.

There are many different magazines to choose from. Some are international, regional, or even local if you live in a large city or municipality. There are also specialty magazines that are dedicated to certain theme weddings or destination weddings. If this is something you will be including in your business then you should have access to these publications. These magazines can be expensive, so choose carefully. Remember, you can look at these for free at a bookstore or, even better, at a library. More than likely you will have one or two favorites to which you will wish to subscribe. Here is a list of the more well-known publications:

Modern Bride — This is published six times a year, and it is focused on brides in their 20s. This magazine offers some good tips on wedding planning, and they provide a fresh perspective on how to plan weddings. This magazine boasts fantastic dresses for every bride's budget and in the latest styles. In addition, they offer tips for planning receptions and romantic honeymoon ideas. This is a good magazine to get a newly engaged bride to help generate ideas about her upcoming wedding. *Modern Bride* also offers 16 special state magazines. The cost for a one-year subscription is about $12.

Brides — This is also one of the top magazines. It is also offered six times a year and is quite large. It is similar to *Modern Bride* and offers many of the same features. This is another great resource for both wedding consultants and the brides they work with.

Elegant Bride — This is the third in the triad of top magazines. They are published by Condé Nast publications and so they are similar in nature. You can check out all three at **www.brides.com**.

Vows **Magazine** — This magazine has been on the scene for about 18 years. It is a magazine for those in the wedding industry. Its focus is the day-to-day business of weddings. Their articles are geared toward issues of bridal retail, how to survive as an independent retailer, how to market your wedding industry business, how to advertise, as well as identifying fashion and consumer shopping trends and preferences. This is a great magazine for a wedding consultant and the business aspects involved. Their Web site is **www.vowsmagazine.com**.

Licenses and Training Involved

Another way you can get started down the path of becoming a wedding consultant is to get some formal training. Here is a small list of Internet sites that can offer you some training on how to become a wedding consultant. This book focuses on the business aspects of becoming a successful wedding consultant. These courses can help fill in the rest.

- **http://www.superweddings.com/weddingconsulting.html** — This site offers training on how to become a certified wedding planner. The site offers a monthly payment program. It was developed by a well-known wedding consultant, Linda Kevich.

- **http://www.acpwc.com** —This is the home page for the Association of Certified Professional Wedding Consultants (ACPWC). This national organization states that they are the primary registered training and certification program for wedding consultants. The course they offer is registered with the Department of Consumer Affairs. They offer a five-day personalized training course and a three-day extended weekend class. They also have seminars and a home study program for wedding consultants. They offer classes at different location nationwide. The fee for the five-day program is $795 and it costs $650 for the home study program.

- **http://www.pennfoster.edu** — This is the home page for the Penn Foster Career School. This school offers an at-home wedding consultant program. Graduates of the program take the Association of Bridal Consultants certification exam.

- **http://www.ashworthuniversity.edu/info** — This online university offers a diploma in bridal consulting.

- Founded in 1955, the Association of Bridal Consultants (ABC), **www.bridalassn.com,** is an international trade association that supports 2,400 members, and offers three professional designations: Professional Wedding Vendor, Accredited Wedding Vendor, and

Master Wedding Vendor. To progress to the top level can take up to six years. They offer a home study program which costs about $400.

❤ Based near San Francisco is June Wedding, Inc., online at **www.junewedding.com.** This association was created for event professionals. Wedding consultants can be awarded the June Wedding, Inc. Certification when they complete the two-part JWI Consultant Training & Certification Home Study Course. This course includes "Setting Up, Designing, and Running a Successful Wedding Consultant/Event Coordination Company," and "Continuing Education for the Advanced Wedding Consultant." The cost for each part of the course is $1,000.

❤ The National Bridal Service offers a home-study program for consultants who are interested in starting a business or increasing their knowledge. You can find information about their program at **www.weddingsbeautiful.com**. When a consultant completes coursework, they receive a certified wedding specialist certificate. The cost for this certification is $695.

These are just of few of the wedding consulting schools and programs available. If you really want to pursue this type of education and certification, you should do your homework. Ask for real-life testimonials from people that have completed their program. You can ask for an address, e-mail address, or phone number. Legitimate programs usually will provide you with this type of information. Most states do not require any special license to be a wedding consultant, but you may wish to check out your state laws before trying to set up a practice. Later in this book, we will talk more about the legal and business aspects of owning and running your own wedding consulting business.

A consideration you should make before taking the leap into being a wedding consultant is to determine if this is going to be a part-time hobby or a full-time job. If you are considering quitting your day job, consider having about four to six months' worth of your salary in savings. It takes about three years for a business to start turning a significant profit, so you need to be prepared for some lean times in between.

Involving Your Community

There are some ways to get positive press. One is to write a press release for the paper. This lets the community know you exist and what you have to offer. It looks like a news story rather than an advertisement and this gives you a little more credibility in the community. Another bonus is that it is free. Editors may use the release as an idea generator for a larger article, which could be even more beneficial to your budding wedding consulting business. There is no guarantee that it will be published, but it is worth the effort. You can also send press releases to local radio and television stations. You never know, you could be contacted for an interview, or at least it can be listed on their community board. Here is a sample of a news release. Make sure it is clear and straight to the point. Make it brief so that it will actually be published. It should not be more than two pages long. If it is more than one page, you need to write the word "more" at the end of the first page. You can include any comments from satisfied clients or any quotes from you about what you do — as if it were an interview.

Your release should be able to answer the basic who, what, why, when, and how. Make sure the information that is most important appears in the beginning of the article.

SAMPLE PRESS RELEASE

XYZ Wedding Consultants

Press Release — For Immediate Release

Loreena and Sarah Brown Open a New Wedding Consulting Business

XYZ Makes Wedding Days a Breeze

Taylorsville, NC – 1/1/2008 – XYZ Wedding Consultants today announced they are open for business for brides planning their weddings. Collectively, Sarah and Loreena have planned and serviced over 300 weddings and receptions. They are knowledgeable about all areas of planning and decorating. Sarah has a Bachelor of Science (B.S.) in hospitality management and a minor in interior design. She has

SAMPLE PRESS RELEASE

been a wedding consultant for over four years and has received her certification in Wedding Planning from the National Association of Wedding Consultants (NAWC) and Professional Wedding Planners. Loreena has a Masters of Business Administration (MBA) and a B.S. in interior decorating and design. Loreena also received her certification from the NAWC and has been a wedding planner for three years. They are offering a number of wedding packages from helping on the day of the wedding to inclusive packages.

They offer services that allow brides and their families to relax and enjoy their wedding. They have the expertise to get the job done and offer services to pamper the bride as well as honeymoon, reception, and rehearsal dinner planning.

To set up an appointment today call 828-555-5555 or send an e-mail to Loreena or Sarah at XYZweddings@weddings.com.

###

To editor — Contact Information:

Sarah Brown 828-555-1000

Here are some important areas to look at in your release. In the example, you will notice that it says "immediate release." This should be included, or if there is a specific date and time, then these need to be at the top of your release.

Next is your name at the bottom and where the editor should be able to reach you. You should emphasize that it is for the editor only so that they do not print your personal information.

Your headline should state exactly what the release is about. In this example it is "Loreena and Sarah Brown Open a New Wedding Consulting Business."

It is a clear message on what the release is about. It should be bold so that it catches the eye of the reader. "XYZ Makes Wedding Days a Breeze" is the subheadline and captures the interest of the reader. This can be a quote.

The next item is the dateline. In the example, it is Taylorsville, NC — 1/1/2008. This allows the reader to know where this is occurring and when.

Make sure you look over your release and have someone else help you edit it. Common reasons that releases are not published are typos, the information is incomplete, or it arrives too late to publish.

If you are not sure that you can do a good release, you could hire a freelance writer to do it for $50-$100. You can find these kinds of writers on **www.elance.com** or **www.guru.com**.

Once you have created your press release you may have to do a little research. You need to find the appropriate person to send your release to. You can do this research on the Internet to find out who the editor of a magazine or newspaper is. If you are still not sure, call the paper, radio, or television station and ask who you need to direct your press release to.

You can also use press releases for any community services or charity events that you might be involved in. If you are doing a celebrity wedding, even if it is a local celebrity, that is a good time to send a press release.

Another way to involve the community is to offer opportunities for interns or volunteers to help you set up and plan weddings. They are learning the wedding trade and you are offering a service to the community. It does not hurt that it is a way to get help free.

If there is any way you can give back to the community in the name of your business by offering discounted services to organizations or charities, this again offers you a way to get your name out while giving back. Many times charities are looking for door prizes, raffle items, or items for silent auctions. Offer a package for these types of events and you will have your name and service associated with these events in their literature free and it gives the community the idea that your business is community and civic minded.

Advertising

As part of your business plan and your marketing efforts, you should be able to focus on who your target audience will be. So how do you reach these brides? The following are some suggestions.

Newsletters

This can be monthly, semiannual, or yearly in frequency. Or it can be just a standard one you send out to the public to explain who you are and what you do. It can contain facts about weddings and some tips about planning, especially hiring a wedding consultant.

If you have a regular newsletter, you can have a focus on different aspects as they correlate to the services you offer, such as theme weddings, honeymoons, or catering.

A newsletter differs from a brochure in that it offers information and tips rather than just information about your business. You can send newsletters to potential or new clients. The information contained will be helpful and give suggestions of other services you offer that the bride had not originally thought of. When discussing an aspect of your services, it is important that you include your fees and schedule you need to perform them.

Here is a list of desktop publishing programs and their average prices:

- ♥ Art Explosion Publisher Pro: $90

- ♥ PagePlus: $30

- ♥ Print Shop Pro Publisher: $95

- ♥ Microsoft Publisher: $150

- ♥ Print Shop: $45

- ♥ Print Shop Essentials: $15

- ♥ Publishing Studio: $100

- ♥ Design & Print: $40

- ♥ Print Workshop: $20

More expensive does not mean better. Make sure that you are printing it on good stock paper and using a decent printer. If not, then have it printed by a professional such as FedEx Kinko's. You need to consider the price of ink in your printer, the cost of paper, and your time when making your decision.

Try to keep your newsletter to two to four pages. You can use the front and back to save money on paper and postage. Make it bright and eye-catching. Make sure your information is easy to find. If you do not have the time, you can seek out a freelancer from Elance.com or Guru.com to do it for you. It will cost $200 or more depending how elaborate you want it.

Brochures

These are relatively inexpensive, especially if you get them printed in larger quantities. These should be strategically placed in places where brides will frequent: bakeries, caterers, florists, men's formal shops, and women's formal shops. Also include locations for wedding dresses, wedding venues, and where wedding cakes are made. On the brochure will be your company name and logo (we will discuss your logo in Chapter 4). You can have a picture on the front, but it should be of a happy wedding scene such as a couple exchanging rings. Your picture does not belong on the front. Inside it should include the following information:

- ♥ What services and packages you offer

- ♥ The cost of the basic services

- ♥ Positive comments from satisfied clients

On the last page you may include a picture of yourself. You should, however, include all of your contact information on the last page. A simple brochure can be trifolded. That gives you six pages to work with. This style also fits nicely into an envelope. You can create your own brochure and use your equipment at home. Make sure you use a good printer and paper. If it looks cheap, people will not take you seriously. You can have it designed by a freelancer if you wish. You should also consider having it printed professionally.

Your brochure is one of the strongest and most important marketing tools you will have at your disposable. It should represent everything you and your company stand for. Make sure you distribute them in as many places as you can. When you are at a vendor's place of business, you can offer to send business their way if they will allow you to display your brochure or at least your business card. You can buy small holders at an office supply store. These keep them neat and add a touch of professionalism.

Blogs

Blogs are the newest way to talk to people. There are sites that cater to certain types of blogs or you can place your blog in certain categories.

Once you get the hang of it, writing a few paragraphs every day or every few days can be done quickly. In this venue you can talk about trials and successes. You can give brides advice about what works in a wedding. Just make sure you are always advertising your services and describe how you can help brides reduce their stress. Explain how your services make the day and the days preceding the day so much more pleasurable for the bride and her family.

You can talk about trends and help your vendors by mentioning them and their services. If your vendors have a blog ask them to return the favor.

Millions of people are reading blogs. The numbers increase daily. So why not use this free venue? Here are some services to consider using — some sites will charge a small fee to use their blog service.

- ♥ **www.blogger.com** — This is a service that is owned by Google. You can set up your free blog or for more exposure you can pay a fee. This is one of the most popular blog sites in use.

- ♥ **www.typepad.com** — This is another very popular site. A fee is imposed after their free trial.

- ♥ **www.bravenet.com** — A popular blog site that is free to use.

♥ **www.myspace.com** — This is a site where you can have your own Web page and blog. There are a lot of young people that frequent here but it is still a good place to put a blog.

If you have a Web site you can also blog there or have a link from your Web site to a blog you have with another service. People do read these, so the effort is worth it.

Magazines and Newspapers

You should invest your advertising dollars in large magazines like *Brides, Modern Bride,* or *Elegant Bride.* Statistics show that only about 1 percent of the population is considering marriage so you need to go to the source.

The cost for magazines is much higher than in the local newspaper, although large publications such as the *New York Times* can be very cost prohibitive. Your ad would be lost in this kind of periodical so it is not the best use of your resources.

If you are going to advertise in a magazine, consider buying a package of advertisements rather than just one. You can get a better rate and you will generate more interest among readers if they see your ad more than once.

You can create the ad yourself using a desktop program or you can hire a freelancer from sites such as **Elance.com** or **Guru.com**.

This is an example of an advertisement created for Exquisite Events.

Mass E-mails

You can use different services online that will give you lists of emails to send advertisements to. This costs a little money, but could be worth the investment. Look for companies that will offer mail lists according to certain demographics such as location, age, and wedding interests. In your e-mail explain your service and how to contact you. Many servers will bounce these e-mails if they are not formatted in the correct way. There are software programs such as the one found at **www.icontact.com.** The Internet is a growing resource for shopping and advertising.

Bridal Shows

I have mentioned the importance of attending and participating at bridal shows throughout this book. Their importance cannot be overemphasized. You will have the maximum exposure for the least amount of money. That is not to say that setting up a booth is free. On average the fees can range from $600-$1500. Do not be fooled by how much they are charging for a booth to determine what type of a show it is or whether it is worth your time. Factors such as attendance are much better indicators of whether a show is right for you or not.

There may be hidden fees associated with a booth you will want to know about. Some venues charge extra for power at the booth and may only have a few booths that have access to power. These are the kind of questions you need to ask before you book a show. If there is power at the booth you need to ask what the rules are and how many outlets are available at each booth. You want to make sure that you have enough power outlets for any equipment you plan to bring.

One important question you need to ask is if a table will be provided, or if it costs extra. You may need to bring one of your own. Of course the next question should be about the dimensions of the booth so that you bring the right table. Some shows will rent tables for vendors, but you need to ask about charges for this service.

Do you need to provide your own sign or will the venue provide this? It is recommended that you bring your own because yours should include your logo and information in large lettering so that people can read it.

Ask the show promoter about the rules concerning handing out materials. Is this limited to your own booth or can people distribute their information anywhere? Nothing can be more bothersome than another wedding consultant handing out his or her information right in front of your booth. Yes, this can and does happen.

The location of your booth is very important. You may want to consider asking the bridal show promoter to show you a layout of the booths and where you would be located. Sometimes the prime locations can cost more. You should ask them to show you who is next to you. It is far better to be with florists or dressmakers than right in the middle of other wedding consultants. Another thing to try to find out is if any of the vendors next to you will be using a PA system, or will have loud music. You do not want to be close to that because you will not be able to talk to people clearly and will miss opportunities. Try to determine where the most traffic will be for the maximum exposure. Booking your place as early as possible will provide you with more options.

The size of the booth will also affect the price. At most shows the smaller exhibitors — less expensive booths — are placed on the outside edge of the room, and the vendors with large booths will be in the center.

Another area to avoid is the concession area. Patrons will often leave trash at your booth or may be standing and eating while blocking others from getting to your booth.

To help you decide whether or not a particular show is worth the money they are charging for a booth, consider these factors:

♥ How large is their average attendance? This can be found on their Web site or literature. You can always ask the event planner.

❤ What services do they offer at the venue for the vendors for the price?

❤ What is the space size you will get for the price?

❤ Where would the location of your booth be?

❤ What are the rules and restrictions at the show? Are there limits on what you can sell or hand out? Are there restrictions concerning your booth?

❤ Do you get electrical hookups at your booth?

❤ Is the venue within your chosen demographic? Will it be attracting the people that will be potential clients?

❤ Does the show provide a table or will you have to bring your own?

When you have decided that you are going to work at a bridal show, you need to begin your preparations. The more organized you are, the more enjoyable and lucrative your experience will be. One of the first things you need to figure out is what your budget will be. You can spend a lot of money quickly on a booth, so it is better if you plan ahead and set a definitive budget. Here are some things to consider when coming up with a budget:

❤ Is there traveling involved and how much will it cost?

❤ Is the show out of town? Will you need lodging and meals?

❤ What will you be handing out at the show? Cards? Brochures? Newsletters? Will you be giving away small gifts with your information attached?

❤ Will there be other people helping you run the booth? Are they doing it on a volunteer basis or will you pay them? Friends and family are great for this and can help you keep your costs down. If the show charges admission, make sure you have passes for those working with you.

♥ What will the size of your booth be? Will you need material to decorate it with?

♥ What kind of display will you have? Will it be a display behind the booth or a table display?

Once you establish what it is going to cost, begin to start a list of materials you will need. You need to decide how many items you are planning to hand out and make sure you start acquiring them. Make sure everything you plan to give out has your information on it. You should look into different types of displays. There are prefabricated booths with lights and a frame to hang things on. These are easy to set up and break down, but can break your budget. Tabletop displays are much more affordable. You can even buy a trifold poster to place pictures and information on for people to view. These are inexpensive and easy to decorate. They are easy to set up and take down.

On the day of the show, find out how early you can arrive to set up. Some venues allow you to set up the night before a show. Check all of the electrical outlets and make sure they work. If there is a problem let the promoter know right away. If you need to move, make sure that the promoter puts up a sign directing attendees to where they have moved your booth.

No wedding consultant should be without emergency kits. In the case of a bridal show, a tool kit should be part of this kit. Consider having electrical tape, duct tape, safety pins, flashlight, batteries, and whatever you may need in a pinch. See the case studies in this book for ideas of what other wedding consultants have in their emergency kits for weddings.

Make sure you give yourself plenty of time to set up your booth. It should look neat, organized, and eye catching. If it looks like you slapped it together, what message do you think you are sending to brides about their wedding day? Not a very positive one. If you have time, look at what other vendors have done with their booths. You can generate many great ideas for future shows.

If you decide to use a tablecloth, choose a cloth one, not a plastic one. This is a bridal show, not an outdoor picnic. Would you use plastic tablecloths at an indoor wedding? Cloth tablecloths look neat and professional. Make sure your company sign is easily seen. It should be professionally done, not handwritten. It is worth the cost and if done right will last for many shows and events.

You may want to display a video of prior weddings you have done. The screen for viewing needs to be about five to six feet off the ground. This allows the video to be at or just above eye level. The sound should be loud enough to hear, but not loud enough to disturb other booths around you. Music and images are just fine for a video; that way you do not have to worry about people hearing a voiceover. Always remember to keep your booth as neat and professional looking as you can at all times.

After your booth is set up, take a few minutes before the show starts and walk around to meet some of the other exhibitors. Take some time to learn about the services they offer, so you may be able to refer customers to them. In return, they may become an excellent source of referrals for your business.

The doors open and the people rush in. It is time to work. Put on a big smile. Get used to it; you will wear it until the last person leaves at the end of the show.

Try to make eye contact. Allow them to come over and look at your material. Be available to ask questions. Be respectful and courteous at all times. Do not scare them away by coming on too strong. Ask them simple questions and try to start a casual conversation. If you see a ring, mention how beautiful it is. Aha! The door is open to ask about a wedding. Many of the attendees are overwhelmed with information. You should offer to get their information and send them information later. They are often overwhelmed with the materials available at these shows, and a follow-up contact can be more personalized, and show them the extra steps that you are willing to take.

One of the ways to generate a list of people for your list of prospects is to offer a free drawing. Make it something exciting to make them want to spend the time writing down their information. You can offer services or items such as champagne glasses or flowers. Have them write down their information and place it in the bowl. You can ask them to write their name on a mailing list or get a business card from them as you are handing them yours. Make sure you have plenty of clipboards with pens attached. The clipboards makes it easy for them to write their information and having the pen attached will assure it will not walk away, unless you are giving away pens with your information imprinted on them. In that case encourage them to take the pen with them.

On your registration sheet they are filling out, make sure you have a line for a bride to write down her wedding date. This is important because if you are already booked that weekend there is not much use sending out your information to them, unless you want them to pass it on to someone else. You are better off saving the postage in most cases.

Have one or more bowls for them to drop the entries into, depending on the size of your booth. You could use a box instead and cover it with wedding present paper with a slit in the top. This adds to the décor of your booth and it adds a touch of class.

A CD Can Generate Business

Creating your own CD is much less expensive than it used to be. With the right hardware, software, and a creative touch, you can create a CD as a giveaway. On the CD you can put pictures of previous weddings and a rundown of your services and packages. You can spend a little more money and have it done professionally. It is up to you. To create a short CD could cost $500 and up, but the more professional it looks the more impressed the brides will be. Make sure that your information is printed on the outside of the CD so they know how to contact you. You can use this CD in your booth and have it play in a loop.

Try to give your attention to everyone that comes to your booth. Do not spend too much time with one attendee or you could miss other opportunities. You can offer to send them more information or offer to contact them later. This is your time to get a large amount of prospects, not just one or two. Make the money you invested in the booth worth the effort.

Do not be discouraged about slow times or days at an event. This is normal. People may be waiting for a special event or to get off work to come. There will be slow times, but do not pack up. Wait until the end; you never know what can happen. You can ask the promoter what the flow was like in previous years. This can help you decide when and if you need help.

In order to keep your booth clean and professional, do not eat or drink there. If you need a drink, keep it out of sight. Straighten and spruce up your booth during the slow times. Take breaks when you need to and walk around a little. Remember to stand up when people come to your booth. Do not sit, as this looks as if you are not interested in them or that you are not available. Do not have conversations with friends or family when others around, and definitely do not be on your cell phone. This surely will lose you potential business.

If you have help and need to contact them or they need you consider investing in some walkie-talkies. This is especially needed in larger shows.

If you do have others helping you, take the time before the show and go over your strategies, rules, and expectations. It is up to you to educate them about everything concerning your wedding consulting business, including packages, prices, and availability. Make sure you plan breaks for your help so that they are not burned out. If they are volunteering, you need to treat them well, because you may need their help some other time.

Make sure they are the right people to help you. Just because they are a friend or family member does not mean that they are good with people.

It is your choice and your company. A rude helper can really hurt sales for you. They need to be upbeat, helpful, and knowledgeable.

If you have children, a bridal show is not where they need to be. You will spend your time chasing them and keeping them occupied rather than concentrating on sales. Ask a friend or relative to help out, even if you need to pay them. Some shows do not allow small children in the booths, so you need to ask ahead of time.

Remember that the point of setting up for a show is to get a list of potential clients. It is not a good idea to do business at the show. Instead, get their information and figure out a time to contact them. They will wait and you will not be giving them the attention they deserve at a booth and missing other potential sales.

An Attendance List Is a Gold Mine

Some shows will allow you to have a copy of their attendance list. This can make your mailing list grow exponentially. Make sure that when you are registering that you ask if you can have a copy of the list. In addition, ask them when you can expect to get it. You do not want to wait months for it. Once you have worked out the details, make sure it is added to your contract. Do not rely on verbal permission, as this may not be enough later on. Get it in writing. Some promoters will allow you to have a list because your are an exhibitor. Some may charge a fee for the list, while other promoters may not give it to you at all. It is definitely worth asking for.

When the show begins to wind down, traffic may slow down. Do not begin to break down until the show is finished. It may be the last people that can be your greatest sales. If you are breaking down, they will not bother to talk to you. At some shows it states in the contract that you cannot pack up early or you could be fined. Keep working until the last person is gone and the doors are closed.

When the show is complete and you are home is when the real work begins. Start compiling that list of names into a database. Mail them information right away while the information is fresh in their minds. Send them a card, brochure, or newsletter. Put in a short note that you are sending them the information due to their attendance at a bridal show. If you wish you can send a follow-up mailing a few weeks after that. Sometimes this second mailing can be just the thing to spur them into action and give you a call. If you have phone numbers of people to talk to make sure you call them right away. Do not delay. If they are interested then you need to close the sale.

Working bridal shows is a learning process. You will make mistakes and want to change things for the next show you attend. Make sure that you write your ideas and thoughts down right away so you will have them ready for the next planning session.

Every show is a new experience, so do not be too discouraged. Just learn from your mistakes and realize that it may not have been the best show for you to go to. Look for others and ask around to see where vendors or other consultants say the best shows to attend are.

Comparison of Brick-and-Mortar Versus Home-Based

The list below contains a list of equipment that might be needed for two different wedding consulting businesses. The first is XYZ Wedding Consultants. They have a limited budget, and they are starting their business as a modest at-home operation. The second is S&W Wedding Experts, and they have a much larger budget, which includes an office and furniture. Both of these are made up but are used here as examples.

XYZ Wedding Consultants

Office Equipment
    Computer, printer $700
    Scanner $250
    Microsoft Office $350

Intuit QuickBooks $250
Wedding software $30
10 MB digital camera/accessories $900
Phone/voice mail/answering machine $200
Postage meter/scale $25

Office Supplies

Letterhead, envelopes, business cards $250
Miscellaneous supplies (pens, folders, etc.)$100
Computer/copier paper $50
Read/write compact disks $30
Total: $3,135

S&W Wedding Experts

Office Furniture

Desk, chair, file cabinet(s), bookcase $3,000
Rent $2500

Total (including all other items above for just the first month): $8,635

Let us consider that XYZ has many items at home already. All they really need is the postage scale, QuickBooks, and an extra phone; now their total is $475. There is a huge difference because in an office you would have to supply everything. The great thing is that you do not need to have a separate office to become a successful wedding consultant.

Wedding Packages & Options

Chapter 4

There are many different options for wedding packages. Each consultant decides what the packages will be, what they will include, and what they will cost. You need to spend time to research how much a particular package will cost. You can do this in a couple of different ways. The first is to create a mock wedding. Go through every stage of what the wedding will need. Get prices on material, vendors, venues, and everything else that you will include in your price. Remember to use your margin of profit after you have included what it will cost. Also remember that your time is worth money. Do not give it away. Consider how much per hour you will charge and make that a part of your package. Mileage is another item to consider when figuring a price on a package.

The second and perhaps more accurate way to adjust and set your prices is to do some real weddings and see how much they really cost you. Your fees may be too high or low and you can adjust these if you need to. Do not undercut your prices in order to get clients. The quality of the work you do and word of mouth is what will get you more work. Set a price and stick with it.

Here is a sample list of possible packages you can offer your clients:

♥ **All-Inclusive package** — This cover everything from A to Z. It starts at the planning stage and you finish after the last guest leaves. You can also include honeymoon planning as well.

♥ **The "Day Of" package** — This package is designed to help the bride on her day by coordinating vendors, helping with decoration, or whatever else needs to be taken care of.

♥ **Rehearsal Dinner** — This is a one-time event package that sometimes can be combined with the "Day Of" package. You help execute the dinner and festivities.

♥ **The "Big Day" package** — This package includes just the planning aspects of the wedding. You can give recommendations of vendors, colors, designs, and other wedding day details. Once the planning is complete, you are finished.

♥ **Parties** — There are many parties that go along with a wedding: bachelor, bachelorette, breakfast, rehearsal dinner, and engagement parties. These kinds of packages help plan and execute one of more of these parties. They include venue, food, and entertainment coordination.

There are many other types of packages to be considered. Some wedding consultants choose to specialize in the types of wedding packages they offer:

♥ Ethnic, religious, or culturally based (Indian, Jewish, Catholic)

♥ Theme weddings (Gothic, fairy tale, Renaissance)

♥ Destination weddings (weddings in which a trip to a location is involved like Europe or Hawaii)

♥ Military weddings

♥ Same-gender weddings

Each of these types of wedding packages will have special pricing depending on what they offer. In addition to packages you can consider offering à la carte items such as invitations, catering, floral arrangements, conducting the ceremony yourself, or a number of different extras that a bride can add on or buy separately. Make sure you have this pricing available and on your material such as your brochures and Web site.

If you are concerned about what to charge, look at what your competition is doing. Consider the market you are targeting and the area and income level of your potential clients. In the case studies section, you will read about some wedding consultants that were interviewed who share what they are charging for their packages.

Here is a formula that can help you figure out a fair hourly fee:

(The amount you want to make in a year) / 52 weeks/5 days per week x 2.5 (this figure is for other expenses being factored in) = per day; then divide by 8 hours = your hourly rate

Networking Opportunities

Working well with others is important. Building a solid network of supports and vendors can save you time, money, and aggravation. I encourage you to read the case studies in the back of this book. You will soon realize that wedding consultants always have a backup plan and it usually includes having other vendors ready should one fail to show.

Being known in the community and knowing others is a valuable asset to a wedding consultant. It makes doing business and finding new clients much easier. One way to help with your networking efforts is to join your local Chamber of Commerce. Many other small businesses such as yours join and it is a great networking resource. The cost to join is reasonable, but the business you can generate will make it well worth the time and effort. You can help boost your reputation as a small business owner by participating in meetings and events that your Chamber of Commerce sponsors.

You can join other business-related organizations as well. These organizations allow you to meet and socialize with other professional people. Remember to have plenty of business cards and brochures on hand for different events and social activities. You never know when you might need one.

Exposure — Local and Nationwide

In addition to local organizations, there are national wedding consultant organizations that you can join. These give you more national exposure and networking opportunities. As you expand your business, these kinds of contacts can be invaluable. You can also learn from other wedding consultants and offer suggestions to those just starting out. The kind of support you feel being a part of a larger organizations can be a boost.

A way to get local exposure is to look at getting on a local cable or television channel or even a radio station. You might get to be interviewed or offer a segment on a show talking about tips for brides or tricks for weddings. There are many shows on television now that are concerned with weddings and even feature different wedding consultants nationwide.

Here are three of the main professional wedding consultant organizations in the United States. There are many other regional and state organizations that can be found on the Internet.

- ♥ Association of Bridal Consultants, **www.bridalassn.com** — This organization offers training for wedding consultants. They have a newsletter, local state chapters, insurance, information about wedding consulting, brochure design critique, advertising, referral service, seminars, an annual conference, and a membership listing.

- ♥ Association of Certified Professional Wedding Consultants, **www. acpwc.com** — This organization offers training, local chapters around the country, a member forum online, and a newsletter.

- ♥ SuperWeddings, **www.superweddings.com** — This organization offers advice, training, certification, and resources for wedding consultants. They have a question-and-answer forum that is moderated by SuperWeddings founder Linda Kevich.

Conducting Business Legally

You can do everything right and still have someone trying to sue you. Whenever you work in a job that involves people in the public sector, you are open to a lawsuit. That does not mean you have done anything wrong; it just means that you are vulnerable.

Sometimes it can be because something went wrong with a vendor, or that it rained at an outdoor wedding. Someone has to be blamed and it could be you.

You should always think ahead and try to protect yourself. In Chapter 2, you learned about liability insurance. This helps protect you so that not everything you own will be taken from you, including your car and home.

The other thing you should think about doing from the beginning is retaining an attorney. It is better to be prepared than caught unawares.

Hiring an attorney can be expensive. Their rates can range from $100 to $500 an hour, or even more in some parts of the country. Some attorneys will require a fee for a consultation, some will not. Most attorneys will ask for a retainer fee to begin working for you. This fee will be held against the money that will be charged for any work they may do for you.

It may be smart to buy into prepaid legal services. This is an account for which you pay an annual fee and they offer services, such as consultations, referrals, contract consultation, and even reduced rates should you need the assistance of an attorney.

So how do you choose the right attorney? One good way is to ask others about whom they use and trust. Try to find a lawyer that deals with small businesses like yours and is familiar with lawsuits and other issues that could arise during the course of normal business. Consider how long they have been in practice and how much courtroom and litigation experience they have. When you talk with them, have a list of questions you want answered. Hiring an attorney is a huge investment and you need to make sure that you are investing the money wisely.

You should never do anything that you think could be illegal, such as setting up a bar at a party without the proper licenses. Since you are handling the planning, this becomes your responsibility. Remember you have more to lose than just your business, you could lose your home and freedom.

Conducting Business Ethically

Your reputation is everything in the wedding planning business. People are trusting you to take care of the most important day in their lives. You must do everything in the most ethical way possible. What you may gain today might lose you everything tomorrow.

There are many ways that you may think you will come out ahead such as cheating on your taxes, charging for items you did not supply, or selling lower-quality items for a higher price in order to increase your profit. These are not only unethical, but they are illegal.

Even if you are not arrested or sued, your reputation will be ruined and your business will fail. It just is not worth it to act in any way that would cause clients to not trust you. The same is true with the vendors you deal with. Make sure you deliver what you promise on a contract. While they may not have enough money or resources to sue you for breach of contract, you will have burned a bridge that can have negative effects beyond a particular vendor.

Business Logo

Unless you are an artist and have some skills, it is recommended that you have a professional create a logo for you. This symbol will go on everything that you do. Some of the wedding consultants in the case studies at the end of this book relate that getting a logo done was one of the largest expenses in starting their company, but it was also one of the most important. It represents who you are and what you do.

Do not use clip art or something you find in a program or on the Internet. More than likely, another consultant is already using that symbol or it may be copyrighted. When you have it developed, get a black-and-white and a color version. Color graphics do not always translate well to black and white so it is better that you have both color and black-and-white versions. You should have different sizes made for you. When you try to shrink or enlarge a graphic you sometimes lose the clarity of it.

The logo should represent you, the company, your tastes, and the message you are trying to convey. Spend some time and think about it before you have it made.

Promotions

Everyone likes to think that he or she is getting a bargain. You can advertise promotional deals for limited times in newspaper or magazines. You can even offer a deal if they mention the ad. This helps you when you are deciding whether a particular marketing strategy is working for you.

Since you are selling a service instead of a product, your promotions should surround getting a little bit extra service for the price. Choose things that will not cost you a lot to give away such as planning a wedding day breakfast as an extra when they buy a particular package. It creates the idea that if a bride chooses you they will get a little extra than what your competition is offering. This strategy does not work when it is overused. If people see the same promotion all the time, they will not feel that they are getting anything extra, or that they should be motivated to act quickly and call you.

IRS

Chapter 5

Never underestimate the IRS. Their job has created a rather complicated web of laws, rules, and forms even for small business owners like you. If you have your accounts in order at tax time, the process will be much quicker and smoother. It is always better to do it correctly the first time. Do not wait until tax time to start thinking about taxes. If you have kept up with your financial records when it comes time to fill out the forms, it should be a breeze. The forms are mostly about plugging in numbers from your profit and loss statement and income and expense ledgers.

Business Permits and Licenses

Depending on where you live, you will need a business permit or license. If you do not have the proper permits, you could be conducting business illegally. Most areas require at minimum a county or city license. This is true even if you are conducting business out of your home. In addition to the local licensing, there may be local, county, state, or federal licensing requirements as well. The good news is the fees for these types of permits are usually cheap. You may run into problems with zoning issues if you are conducting a business in an area zoned as residential. Do not try to conduct business without these permits or you could be fined, or worse, arrested. In some cases you can get a zoning variance from the municipal planning commission since your type of work will not increase the traffic in an area.

You might have another business such as cake baking that will require a permit from a health inspector. If you are planning on doing major renovating or remodeling at your house to make a home office, you may be required to get a building permit.

As a wedding consultant, you will not need to get a federal license unless you decide to serve alcohol or engage in some activity that is regulated by the government.

You should go to city hall or the county courthouse or call the clerk's office to find out where you need to go to get a permit, what you will need to bring, and what the fees will be.

What Is a Federal ID Number? Do I Need One?

In certain cases the federal government may require a small business to have an Employment Identification Number (EIN). You will need one if you choose to have any kind of business other than a sole proprietorship. If you plan to work independently and have no one else working for you in your wedding consulting business then you can use your social security number as your identification number for tax purposes. If not you must apply for an EIN from the IRS.

In the application for your EIN you will notice that the IRS requires you to declare a fiscal year start and end. Certain states also require in their certificate of incorporation that you declare when your fiscal year begins. Most companies make the calendar year the same as their fiscal year. The second most popular choice is July 1 to June 30.

If you decide to incorporate, you will have to file two returns. For the first half of the year, you will file an individual return as a sole proprietor using

Schedule C and any other schedules that are indicated. After the second half of your year, you will file a corporate return. You have a couple of choices; you can file a Form 1120, or Form 1120S if you make a Subchapter S election. You will also file an individual return, because you will be an employee of your own corporation.

There are some variations of this. If you choose April 1 to October 1 as the beginning of your fiscal year, then you will be filing the same two sets of returns. However, if you choose April 1, you will file as a sole proprietor for the first quarter, which runs January 1 to March 31. Then you will file corporate and individual returns for the last three quarters — April 1 to December 31.

If October 1 is the beginning of your fiscal year, you will file as a sole proprietor for the first three quarters, which are January 1 to September 30. You will then file corporate and individual returns for the last quarter, which runs October 1 to December 31.

There is a benefit to declaring a separate fiscal year. It allows you more freedom in your tax planning. The savings that you and your account can develop through this freedom of planning can be significant. You should speak to an accountant or tax professional to decide which fiscal year will benefit you the most. In addition, you will have fewer tax forms to file.

On the other hand, there are some significant disadvantages to choosing a separate fiscal year. You will have to decide what the best plan is for you. As a sole proprietor, you may just wish to stick with having your fiscal year follow your calendar year.

The IRS as Your Tax Information Source

The laws change frequently, and if an agent is not current on tax laws, he or she may not be very helpful. You can find the information you need from a selection of different IRS publications:

Some helpful publications that the IRS offers are free. The IRS wants you to do your taxes right because they want their money, so try to use what they have to offer, especially if it is free. Any forms or publications you get from their Web site will be the most up-to-date forms available.

For information concerning starting a business and keeping records, Publication 583 is a good source of information. This can be retrieved from **http://www.irs.gov/pub/irs-pdf/p583.pdf**.

For a good reference guide when figuring out what taxes you need to pay and when, consider reading Publication 334, online at **http://www.irs.gov/pub/irs-pdf/p334.pdf**.

Publication 509 will help you find answers about tax calendars when certain taxes are due. This can be retrieved from **http://www.irs.gov/pub/irs-pdf/p509.pdf**.

As a small business you may need to pay estimated taxes and Publication 505 may help answer some of your questions. This can be retrieved from **http://www.irs.gov/pub/irs-pdf/p505.pdf**.

Almost every IRS form is available online in pdf format. For others you may need, simply go to **http://www.irs.gov** and type "Form" along with the number in the search bar near the top.

Self-Employment Tax

In addition to other taxes, as a sole proprietor, partnership, or as an LLC, if you make more than $400 you have to pay self-employment(SE) tax. If you have to pay this then you will file it on the Form 1040 Schedule SE. This is available at **http://www.irs.gov/pub/irs-pdf/f1040sse.pdf**.

You should set aside money to pay your taxes. A good amount to start off with is 20 to 25 percent. If you have anything left over at tax time you can reinvest it as a capital investment fund or a bonus. You can build an account dedicated to paying taxes. If you do not touch this you can save yourself from scrambling for money later. This money can also pay for your Social Security and Medicare payments. So it is important that you save and plan ahead.

Accounting Issues

There are a number of accounting programs such as Microsoft Office Small Business Accounting and QuickBooks. These are great programs to invest in. They will help you keep up with your finances, especially when it comes to tax time.

You can also use these programs and then upload the information to an accountant. This can be very helpful to both of you. If you want to be low tech, a simple written ledger would be necessary.

Either of these forms of accounting will only work if you are putting the information into them that is needed. You have to set time aside every day or at least every few days to input your invoices, payments, and bills. If you are not diligent in entering this information, you can fall behind or miss something. This can cost you money.

Keep all of your receipts and invoices in one place. Invest in a small filing cabinet with file folders. Do not keep receipts and papers all over your house. Keep a clean and organized office. You will thank yourself later. Running a business is not just about doing weddings; you have to spend the time doing the business end as well.

Outside Vendors and How They Can Help

If you have employees, make sure that you have a solid understanding of employee taxes, as these can be the trickiest taxes to deal with. You may come to a point in your wedding consulting business that you will want to hire more employees. From a secretary to a person to help you set up a venue, you need to be prepared to commit 30 percent of your payroll to taxes and paperwork. It will be your responsibility to withhold all of your full- or part-time employees' federal and state income tax, Social Security, and Medicare taxes from paychecks. At tax time, you will need to remit them with your overall tax bill. In addition, you will have to pay your company's portion of Social Security and Medicare benefits. You must consider that with employee salaries up to $87,922 you can expect to be taxed 6.2 percent for Social Security and 1.45 percent for Medicare.

Social Security and Medicare taxes pay for benefits that workers and families receive under the Federal Insurance Contributions Act (FICA). Social Security tax pays for benefits under the old age, survivors, and disability insurance part of FICA. Medicare tax pays for benefits under the hospital insurance part of FICA. You have to pay your portion of your employees' taxes that matches what you have withheld from them. You should use Form 941 to file the federal, Social Security, and Medicare taxes.

In addition to these taxes, you will also be responsible for Federal Unemployment Tax Act (FUTA) taxes. You have to pay this separately from other taxes. Your employees do not pay into this tax. You are totally responsible for it. This is another thing to consider before hiring others to work as employees in your wedding consulting business. You will need to file a Form 940 to cover the FUTA taxes.

Make sure that you deposit the taxes in a financial institution that is able to hold these types of funds.

Here is the calendar of when payroll taxes are due:

- April 15 for wages paid January through March

- July 31 for April through June

- October 31 for July through September

- January 31 for October through December

If you owe more taxes than $500, then your due date changes to the fifteenth day of the next month.

INDEPENDENT CONTRACTOR AGREEMENT

This agreement is made on _____, 20 _____, between_ _____, owner, of _____ _____, City of _____, State of _____, and _____ _____, contractor, of _____ _____, City of _____, State of _____.

For valuable consideration, the owner and contractor agree as follows:

1. The independent contractor agrees to furnish all of the labor and materials to do the following work for the owner as an independent contractor:

2. The contractor agrees that the following portions of the total work will be completed by the dates specified:

3. The contractor agrees to perform this work in a professional manner according to standard practices. If any plans or specifications are part of this job, they are attached to and are part of this agreement.

4. The owner agrees to pay the contractor as full payment $_____ for doing the work outlined above. This price will be paid to the contractor on satisfactory completion of the work in the following manner and on the following dates:

5. The contractor and the owner may agree to extra services and work, but any such extras must be set out and agreed to in writing by both the contractor and the owner.

6. The contractor agrees to indemnify and hold the owner harmless from any claims or liability arising from the contractor's work under this agreement.

INDEPENDENT CONTRACTOR AGREEMENT

7. No modification of this agreement will be effective unless it is in writing and is signed by both parties. This agreement binds and benefits both parties and any successors. This document, including any attachments, is the entire agreement between the parties. This agreement is governed by the laws of the State of _____.

Dated:_____, 20 _____

_____
Signature of Owner

_____
Printed Name of Owner

_____
Signature of Contractor

_____
Printed Name of Contractor

_____
Address

_____
EIN or Social Security Number

There is another option you may want to consider instead of hiring employees, and that is hiring independent contractors. Hiring independent contractors can save you paperwork and expenses. As a wedding consultant, you will be more likely to hire these types of workers as you need them for different weddings and celebrations. Having a list of independent contractors is a good thing to develop. Sometimes different vendors can be classified as independent contractors as well.

The definition of an independent contractor is a worker that is in business for himself and who pays his own taxes and insurance. Independent contractors will use their own equipment or facilities. One of the benefits of hiring independent contractors is that they require little or no supervision, and they are typically paid per wedding.

There are some definite things you must consider when determining whether a worker is an employee or an independent contractor. This assists you in avoiding the threat of tax fraud and liability charges. You must make sure that the above factors apply to them and that these points are clear to the workers.

You should be sure that you are using an independent contractor and not treating him or her as an employee. If you make a mistake, you could be liable for employment taxes for that worker and in addition, you may be fined a penalty.

One of the best ways to ensure that you do not make any errors in utilizing independent contractors is to develop and use a written independent contractor's agreement. On the previous page is a sample of an independent contractor's contract. You can also find a copy of it on the CD. Be sure that you include the contractor's full name, address, and social security number or EIN.

A bonus of using an independent contractor is that you do not have to withhold or pay any taxes on payments you make to them. They are responsible for their own taxes. A gauge that is generally used with an independent contractor is that the person for whom the services are performed has the right to control or direct only the result of the work and not what will be done and how it will be done or the method of accomplishing the result.

Many of the vendors you will work with, such as florists, caterers, party suppliers, musicians, and bartenders are generally not employees. However, whether such people are employees or independent contractors is determined on a case-by-case basis. Independent contractors are subject to self-employment tax. You will need to make sure that all of your independent contractors complete an FDIC Substitute Form W-9 Request for Taxpayer Identification Number and Certification. This form provides the independent contractor's correct taxpayer identification number to you. You will be required to file a Form 1099-MISC, Miscellaneous Income, to report payments of $600 or more to persons who are independent contractors you may use in the course of a wedding.

You can get a W-9 form by visiting **http://www.irs.gov/pub/irs-pdf/fw9. pdf**.

Confidentiality Issues

More than likely you will have to handle any files or information that would be considered confidential. Some clients may ask you to sign a confidentiality agreement. It is always advisable to have an attorney look over anything before you sign it.

You should take every precaution to protect your client's privacy. This is just good business practice. That means that you should not be gossiping about what you saw or heard at a wedding. Your credibility can be severely damaged by idle gossip.

You should be careful not to send information such as credit card information, social security numbers, dates of birth, or any other personal information over the Internet. It is just too vulnerable and can be stolen and used. If you have any of the information in your files and need to purge those records, make sure that they are shredded. There are a number of good shredders that can be bought at places that sell office supplies. All of your receipts, contracts, bills, and anything else that has identifying information should be shredded, not just thrown away. Crooks will go through dumpsters to find personal information to use illegally.

Desktop Programs That Can Help

There are a few programs that can help you keep up with your finances.

♥ **Quicken** — This program comes in a few different versions, and basically acts like an electronic checkbook. The great thing is that you can download you balances from online and use the information to help you at tax time, since the information can be downloaded in some tax software. If you have kept good records and put items in appropriate categories, finding deductions will be a snap.

💜 **Tax Cut** — This program is created by H&R Block. It asks you questions and you fill in the data based upon your records. They also have state versions that download the information you input for your federal return. You can file your taxes electronically for a fee.

💜 **TurboTax** — This is another popular program that offers many of the same features that Tax Cut does. Each program costs about $40. If you are comfortable doing your own taxes, either of these programs will be helpful.

Filing Taxes as a Business

If you are a sole proprietor and do not have any employees, pay no excise tax, and did not inherit the business, you may be able to use your social security number for tax purposes. If you do not fit these requirements then you will be required to get a federal Employer Identification Number (EIN).

Is Your Wedding Consulting a Business or a Hobby?

You should decide early on whether your wedding consulting is a hobby or a business. It will make a difference when it comes to your taxes. The difference between a job and a hobby is that you do not expect to make a profit while doing a hobby. If you decide you will not make a profit at wedding consulting there is a limit on the deductions you can take.

On your tax returns you must include any income you make from your hobby. If you just like performing your wedding consulting services for friends and family for fun then you must include this on your tax returns.

If you make a significant profit from it you should not consider it a hobby. On your taxes you cannot use a loss from wedding consulting activities to offset other income. Wedding consulting activities you do as a hobby come under this limit.

The limit on not-for-profit losses applies to individuals, partnerships, estates, trusts, and S corporations. However, this limit does not apply to corporations other than S corporations.

To help you determine whether your wedding consulting business is an activity for profit you should consider the following:

- Do you perform your wedding consulting activities in a businesslike manner?

- Does the time and effort you put into wedding consulting indicate that you intend to make it a profitable venture?

- Do you depend on income you make from wedding consulting as your main source of income and rely on it as your livelihood?

- Are your losses due to circumstances beyond your control or are they normal in the startup phase of your type of business?

- Have you changed your methods of doing business in an attempt to improve your profitability?

- Do you and those that are supporting you have the experience, knowledge, and skills to create a successful business?

- Have you made a profit doing similar activities in the past? What is that profit?

- Does your wedding consulting make some profit some years?

- Do you expect to make a future profit from the appreciation of the assets used in your wedding consulting activities?

Depreciation

Another thing you need to consider when doing your taxes is depreciation. The equipment that you use often ages or becomes obsolete. It is important that you keep clear records of what you buy. If you are using equipment that you bought before you started your wedding consulting business, you may depreciate the equipment based on their market value at the time you began using them for business. Any major repairs and improvements may also be depreciated. The other requirement for being able to depreciate equipment is that it must be used in your wedding consulting business. This may seem obvious, but you cannot use your television in your living room as an asset just because you watched a wedding video on it. You must use the equipment mostly for business purposes. Cell phones are one of these items you must consider. You are better off using a dedicated phone for your business so that there is not any question of whether it can be used as a business asset or not.

Depreciation ends when you have recovered its cost or retired it from service. The kind of property you own affects how you can claim a depreciation deduction. There are two types of property you will have in your business: tangible and intangible.

Tangible property is real property that can be seen or touched. There are two types of tangible property: real property, which is immovable property, and personal property, which is movable property. Examples of real property are buildings and land. Examples of personal property are cars, machinery, or equipment. Certain types of property cannot be depreciated. An example of this is land because it cannot wear out or become obsolete.

In contrast, intangible property is property that cannot be seen or touched. Examples of these assets are copyrights, franchises, or patents. Some of these assets cannot be depreciated, but must be amortized instead. If you have questions on whether to depreciate or amortize, you should use Form 4562, Depreciation and Amortization. You can find the form by visiting the following Web site: **http://www.irs.gov/pub/irs-pdf/f4562.pdf**.

You do have the option of deducting all or part of the cost of certain qualifying property used in your business in the year you placed it in service. You can do this by claiming a Section 179 deduction. The bonus of claiming the Section 179 deduction is that you get to deduct more value of the asset in the beginning. The rule is that you must claim the Section 179 deduction only when your property is ready to be used in your wedding consulting business. For items placed into service in 2008, the maximum deduction is $250,000. This limit is reduced by the amount by which the cost of qualified property placed in service during the tax year exceeds $800,000. Another rule is that you cannot deduct costs in excess of your taxable income. If you decide to use the Section 179 deduction you will need to use Form 4562.

You may also decide not to claim this deduction — perhaps if your taxes will be small due to how your business did that year. In this case you can choose to write the costs according to the depreciation of any or all items with a life of over one year. In this case you will deduct the cost of an item divided over a period of years. The length of this type of depreciation can range from three to 39 years, depending on the type of property you are considering. The larger the amount, the longer the depreciation.

Avoiding an Audit

The simplest way to avoid an audit is to keep good records. Your return must have supporting documentation of any income, expenses, and credits you report. If you kept good records to begin with this should not be a problem. If the IRS decides to audit your tax returns, the auditor may ask you to explain the items reported. Having all your receipts accounted for with complete records can make this a painless, quick process. You should have either electronic or paper accounting journals and ledgers. In these business books you must show your gross income as well as your deductions and credits. Some of the items you should have available are any sales slips, paid bills, invoices, receipts, deposit slips, and canceled checks. After you have filed a return, you should store these records along with a copy of your return in a safe place. A shoebox in your closet may not be a premium location, but as long as you know where the records are and that they are organized, that is fine. A rule of thumb is to keep your taxes and records for at least four years. It is up to you to prove entries, deductions, and statements you made on your tax returns. If you have good records this "burden of proof" should be a snap.

When the four years have elapsed on a particular set of financial records, do not discard them until you check to see if you have to keep them longer for other purposes.

When to Hire an Accountant

If you can afford it, you should try to hire an accountant from day one, especially if you are not good with numbers. You need to be honest with yourself concerning this, because if you do your taxes wrong, you could lose not only your job, but your personal assets as well, especially if you are a sole proprietor. Try to get an accountant that is familiar with wedding consulting. This can be a great benefit because they can get a better working understanding with your business and what kinds of taxes you will owe, as well as specific deductions you can make. If the accountant is familiar with working with a business of your size, he or she can help keep you on track as far as deadlines. An accountant can help you set up any financial software from the beginning. They can set the books up in a way that can better help you run your business.

If you are not sure that you can handle it, or you are not good with numbers, you may consider hiring an accountant or a tax professional. They can help you navigate tax laws as well as find and maximize your deductions.

Even if you decide not to utilize an accountant for ongoing tax preparation, you may consider consulting with one at the beginning in order to establish a financial structure and answer general questions about your finances.

Record Keeping

It is worth the expense to buy good bookkeeping software. Make sure you have a good backup and try to keep hard copies should anything happen. Make sure that your software is kept current, and that it can let you know when and what taxes you need to pay. Make sure that you have a reminder that will let you know when to do certain bookkeeping functions.

So what are the mysterious business expenses you have heard so much about? Can you just call every meal and vacation a business expense? Not exactly.

For an item to qualify as a deduction, expenses must be business related, ordinary, necessary, and reasonable. The best way to keep a close eye on your business expenses is to pay for items from your business account. When you do this, you should make sure to enter your qualifying expenses in the appropriate expense ledger category and keep all receipts. It bears repeating…keep *all* of your receipts.

The correct way to record your expenses is to record what you actually paid out. Do not use the market value. You cannot deduct interest charges on your purchases. If you engage in any type of barter economy, you should know that it is treated like any other business income based on fair market value.

You may have questions about startup costs. Deducting these expenses can be more complicated, and you may want to rely on the advice and assistance of an accountant or tax professional. If you choose to try to tackle business-related startup expenses on your own, realize that startup expenses can be deducted two different ways. The first way is that they may be capitalized at the time you quit or sell your business. The second way is that these costs can be amortized monthly over a 60-month period.

Business deductions can only be deducted if the activity is undertaken with the intent of making a profit. That means if you meet with one of your friends for lunch and they are a caterer, the lunch has to be about making a partnership or to discuss a new wedding project. It cannot be about talking about old times, and how business is going for the both of you. It has to be for the express purpose of making a profit. It is a good idea to write down on the receipt what the purpose of the expense was and make sure you write it in your ledger as well. The longer you wait, the harder it will be to remember.

You cannot necessarily make deductions the first year you are in business. The IRS often states that you have to be making a profit and be a viable business before you can begin making deductions. You can meet this requirement by making a profit in any two years of a five-year period. When you reach this requirement then you can begin deducting business expenses such as supplies, subscriptions to professional journals, and an allowance for the business use of your car or truck.

Since you are working at home, you can make deductions for utilities and, in some cases, even a new paint job on your home if this helps improve your business. But you can only deduct a proportional amount based on the size of your dedicated office. Remember that the IRS is going to treat the part of your home you use for business as if it is a business and not part of the rest of the home. You have to be diligent in making sure you have clear, concise records, and make sure that you do not mix business and personal matters.

In addition to helping you out at tax time, good record keeping can help you to monitor the progress of your business. Good records can show you if your wedding consulting business is growing or failing. It can show you where you need to make improvements and can signal you to make a new market analysis. If you are not attracting the right clients, your figures will show it. The better your records are the greater the chance your consulting business has in succeeding.

All of your financial records should be as accurate as possible. This can help you prevent an audit. In addition, these records can help you when you need to deal with your bank and creditors. Your records should include income — or profit and loss — statements and balance sheets. An income statement will show the income and expenses of your wedding consulting business over a period of time. Your balance sheet will show your assets, liabilities, and equity on any given date. As a wedding consultant you will receive money from many sources and clients. You need to be sure that your records can identify the source of your receipts. That is why writing down who you gave you money, what for, and the date are important. This is the same procedure for any business-related expenses.

What Supplies/Forms Do I Need on Hand?

You must adhere to all reporting and payment schedules set by the IRS. This may vary according to the type of legal structure you have selected for your business. Here is the calendar for sole proprietors and the forms they need to file. This is the schedule that you are most likely to use as a wedding consultant. The ones in italics will only apply if you have employees.

January 15 — Estimated tax filing Form 1040ES

April 15 — Estimated tax filing Form 1040ES

June 15 — Estimated tax filing Form 1040ES

September 15 — Estimated tax filing Form 1040ES

January 31 — Social Security (FICA) tax and income tax withholding Forms 941.

April 30 — Social Security (FICA) tax and income tax withholding Forms 941

July 31— Social Security (FICA) tax and income tax withholding Forms 941.

October 31 — Social Security (FICA) tax and income tax withholding Forms 941.

January 31 — Providing information on Social Security (FICA) tax and the withholding of income tax to employee Form W-2

January 31 — Federal Unemployment Tax (FUTA) Form 940-EZ or 940

January 31 — Federal Unemployment Tax (FUTA) (only if liability for unpaid taxes exceeds $100) Form 8109 to make deposits

April 15 — Federal Unemployment Tax (FUTA) (only if liability for unpaid taxes exceeds $100) Form 8109 to make deposits

July 31 — Federal Unemployment Tax (FUTA) (only if liability for unpaid taxes exceeds $100) Form 8109 to make deposits

October 31 — Federal Unemployment Tax (FUTA) (only if liability for unpaid taxes exceeds $100) Form 8109 to make deposits

January 31 — Statement returns to nonemployees and transactions with other or independent contractors Form 1099 to individuals

February 28 — Statement returns to nonemployees and transactions with other or independent contractors Form 1099 to IRS

April 15 — Income tax filing Schedule C (Form 1040)

April 15 — Self-employment tax filing Schedule SE (Form 1040)

If your fiscal year is not January 1 through December 31:

Schedule C (Form 1040) is due on the fifteenth day of the fourth month after the end of your tax year. Schedule SE is due the same day as income tax (Form 1040). Estimated tax (1040ES) is due on the fifteenth day of the fourth, sixth, and ninth months of the tax year and the fifteenth day of the first month after the end of your tax year.

Now this may seem overwhelming, but not all of these forms will apply to you if you do not have employees or utilize independent contractors.

You may have a partner agreement. If this is the case, here is a sample calendar of what forms you will need and when you will need to file them:

January 15 — Estimated tax filing by individual who is a partner Form 1040ES

April 15 — Estimated tax filing by individual who is a partner Form 1040ES

June 15 — Estimated tax filing by individual who is a partner Form 1040ES

September 15 — Estimated tax filing by individual who is a partner Form 1040ES

January 31 — Social Security (FICA) tax and income tax withholding Forms 941.

April 30 — Social Security (FICA) tax and income tax withholding Forms 941.

July 31 — Social Security (FICA) tax and income tax withholding Forms 941.

October 31 — Social Security (FICA) tax and income tax withholding Forms 941.

January 31 — Providing information on Social Security

(FICA) tax and the withholding of income tax to employee Form W-2

January 31 — Federal Unemployment Tax (FUTA) Form 940-EZ or 940

January 31 — Federal Unemployment Tax (FUTA) (only if liability for unpaid taxes exceeds $100) Form 8109 to make deposits

April 15 — Federal Unemployment Tax (FUTA) (only if liability for unpaid taxes exceeds $100) Form 8109 to make deposits

July 31 — Federal Unemployment Tax (FUTA) (only if liability for unpaid taxes exceeds $100) Form 8109 to make deposits

October 31 — Federal Unemployment Tax (FUTA) (only if liability for unpaid taxes exceeds $100) Form 8109 to make deposits

January 31 — Statement returns to nonemployees and transactions with other or independent contractors Form 1099 to individuals

February 28 — Statement returns to nonemployees and transactions with other or independent contractors Form 1099 to IRS

February 28 — Providing information on Social Security (FICA) tax and the withholding of income tax to employee Forms W-2 and W-3 to the Social Security Administration

April 15 — Income tax filing Schedule C (Form 1040)

April 15 — Annual return of income Form 1065

April 15 — Self-employment tax filing (by individual who is a partner) Schedule SE (Form 1040)

If your fiscal year does not follow the calendar year then income tax is due on the fifteenth day of the fourth month after the end of your tax year.

Schedule SE is due the same day as income tax (Form 1040).

Estimated Tax (1040ES) is due on the fifteenth day of the fourth, sixth, and ninth months of the tax year and the fifteenth day of the first month after the end of your tax year.

This of course is a more complicated set of taxes and dates and forms. This is something to consider *before* you set up a partnership because you might be forced to hire an accountant, and your bookkeeping duties will jump dramatically. So, just when you did not think things could get any more difficult, consider the tax schedule for employees.

When you decide to become a small-business owner and start your own wedding consulting business, you take on a lot of responsibility. The day you decide to hire employees things will change dramatically. First is that you can no longer just use your social security number; you must get a federal EIN.

You must file your employees' federal, state, and local taxes. There is a certain amount of taxes you must withhold from your employees' paychecks. Here is a list of typical taxes you will be responsible for as an employer:

- Federal income tax withholding

- Social Security and Medicare taxes

- Federal Unemployment Tax Act (FUTA)

- Federal income taxes/Social Security and Medicare taxes

In order to figure out how much you must withhold for federal taxes on your employee(s) you should refer use the employee's Form W-4. In order to help you navigate this form, refer to Publication 15, Employer's Tax Guide, and Publication 15-A, the Employer's Supplemental Tax Guide.

Chapter 6

What's in a Name

One of the most important things you will do for your business is pick the right name. A name defines what your business is and what it does. Sometimes wedding consultants pick names that are too cute or have no meaning for them. Your name should be clear and when people see it or hear it they should know immediately what it is and what kind of work you do.

Choosing a Name for Your Business

Choosing the right name may be a daunting task. In fact, it could be the hardest thing you do. It should be a priority early on. It is needed to not only define that you have a business but it is needed for stationery, business permits, tax forms, and much more.

One mistake that many wedding consultants do is to use their name in the name of their business such as "Loreena Brown's Wedding Consulting." While it does define who you are and what you do, it can create a lot of confusion and problems.

First, if a client makes a check out to the business name rather than you, your bank could refuse to cash it. In addition, it can create confusion for the IRS. They may have problems separating you from your business. This is further complicated if you have a home business because the address will be the same. One thing you do not want to do is confuse or attract undue attention from the IRS.

Your name is your moniker and should be classy and instill confidence in your clients. If you get too cutesy with your name, your clients may have a hard time taking you seriously.

If you choose a name with the letter "A" in the beginning it can put you at the top of the list in phone directories or any other kind of business directory. There can be some advantages to this. Your company name should be easy to say and should be easy to spell and remember.

You can have friends and family help you with suggestions. You can make a small contest and offer a small prize for the winning name. Do not be too quick to choose a name. Take your time, sleep on it, and then consider it again. Once you choose it, you could be stuck with it. Not only that, but a bad name could mean bad business. Choose wisely.

Researching Availability of Names

You cannot use just any name. Some names are trademarked. There may be some state regulations in the type of name you may use and the rules may prohibit some specific words from being used in your company name. You should check for state regulations concerning naming a business. You can go to **http://www.uspto.gov** to see if your name has been trademarked. You can also do a Google search of the name and see what comes up. This will be especially important when choosing a domain name for a Web site.

When you choose a name you may want to register and trademark it. You will register it as a DBA "doing business as." This will allow your company to exist as a separate entity from you. This is necessary if you form an LLC but it is a good idea to do even as a sole proprietor. Different states have rules and forms to do this. A good place to go is **http://www.dbaform. com**. Some banks will require this before you can open an account using your business name.

Here is a sample statement to adopt a business name:

FICTICIOUS BUSINESS NAME

Statement of Intention to Conduct Business under an Assumed or Fictitious Name

The undersigned party does hereby state his/her intention to carry on the business of _____ at the business location of _____ in the City of _____ in the State of _____ under the assumed or fictitious name of _____ _____.

The owner's name, home address, and percentage of ownership of the above-named business are as follows:

Name:

Address:

Percentage of Ownership:

Signed on _____ 20 _____.

_____

Business Owner Signature

_____

Business Owner Printed Name

You can choose to trademark your name, but this is not as necessary as a DBA. You can find the necessary forms and information at **http://www. uspto.gov**.

Service Contracts

You should create your service contracts that you use with your clients. If you need help you should consult an attorney familiar with these types of contracts. You need to make sure it answers the five main questions:

♥ **Who** — Who is going to do what work? Who is responsible for what work? Who will pay the consultant?

- 💗 **What** — What work is being promised? This needs to be clear and concise. Add everything, and do not assume anything.

- 💗 **Where** — Where is this work to be done? What are the specific locations?

- 💗 **When** — When is this work to be done? What are the milestones and deadlines for certain items to be completed? When is money to be paid?

- 💗 **How** — What is the expectations of the consultant? Will they be at the wedding the whole time?

This is a sample of a contract that Lili's Concept uses with their clients.

SAMPLE CONTRACT

Service Agreement

This agreement is made on the month of _____ on the day of ____ _____, 2008.

Between: Lili's Concept

      12109 Ridgefield Parkway

      Richmond, VA, 23238

      ("Hereinafter referred to as "Planner")

And: Client (s): _____

      Client Address: _____

      City, State, Zip: _____

      ("Hereinafter referred to as "Client")

For: Wedding and /or Event Planning Services

To describe the terms and conditions under which Lili's Concept will provide certain consulting, design, and implementation services (the "Services") to Client in connection with the client's wedding or event on _____.

Now therefore, in consideration of the foregoing promises exchanged in this agreement, the parties agree as follows:

Sample Contract

1. **Services:** Lili's Concept agrees to perform services for the client as listed in Exhibit A for the _____package. The services are described in Exhibit A attached hereto and incorporated herein by reference. Lili's Concept will provide a budget guide and a wedding checklist to the client. Lili's Concept will also provide a complimentary planner book and a 25% discount on any manufactures listed on the attached sheet.

Planner agrees to provide the following services to the client in consideration of the amount specified in the section titled fees:

Package (includes):

_____
_____
_____
_____

Additional Services Requested:

_____
_____
_____
_____

Service, as described above, to be performed on or about the following date(s):

_____
_____

2. **Client Obligations:** Client will work with Lili's Concept regarding the services to be rendered hereunder, and they will provide any necessary information, including vendor contact information, contact information of guests and wedding party, and dates for Lili's Concept to efficiently perform the services outlined in this agreement.

3. **Fee Schedule**

   Package (# or name): _____

   Initial consultation: _____

   Subsequent consultations: _____

   Vendor visits: _____

   Wedding or event coordination: _____

   Rehearsal coordination: _____

   Total: _____

SAMPLE CONTRACT

The client agrees to the total fee as outlined above and to a payment schedule as follows:

Payment Options and Schedule

Initial payment of 10% for all services under $1,000.00 is due at the time of signing this contract (this payment is nonrefundable).

_____ (initial)

Initial payment of $350.00 for all services over $1,000.00 is due at the time of signing this contract (this payment is nonrefundable).

_____ (initial)

À la carte service fees are due at the signing of contract, unless they are added on to packages.

Option One * Fifty percent of the fee due at signing of contract. In the amount of _____, second payment due one month prior to event.

Final Payment due date is: _____/_____/_____

Option Two * Three-payment plan (after the initial deposit has been paid). Payment will be broken down into three payments due on either the first or fifteenth of noted dates. The first payment will be due in 30 days on: _____/_____/_____. The second payment is due on: _____/_____/_____. Final Payment is due on: _____/_____/_____.

Option Three: * Monthly payment plan (this option is only available for services and or packages over $1,000.00).

Monthly payment plan due on the first or fifteenth of each month. Total of _____ _____( ) payments. Final payment is due on _____/_____/_____.

Option Four * Payment made in full. If client would like to pay in full they may pay at the time of signing this contract, or they may make their initial deposit and pay remaining balance two weeks from that date.

Payment paid in full on _____/_____/_____

Customized Payment Plan

_____

_____

_____

_____

SAMPLE CONTRACT

Late payments will be charged 1.5% per monthly billing cycle (18% APR) for delinquent accounts. Payments that are over six months late will be turned over to a collection agency.

Returned checks will be charged a $35.00 late fee.

4.   Cancellation Policy

Since our services are largely time and planning, we do our best to provide a refund policy that takes this into account. Should you cancel our services or your event, we will provide you a refund as structured below:

In the event the services of Lili's Concept are no longer required (cancellation of event) the client agrees to pay a percentage of the total agreed fee. In the event client cancels services within ninety days of signing contract client will forfeit the initial deposit and be billed at $75.00 per hour for any work that may have been done up to that point. If client cancels anytime after ninety days the client will be charged the initial deposit and 25% of the remaining total. If client cancels thirty days or less prior to the event 100% of the fee will be owed to Lili's Concept.

If planner is unable to attend events, or complete the contract due to illness, tragedy, or force majeure, planner will provide a replacement with capabilities and experience to finish the tasks.

_____ (initial)

5.   Refund Policy

In the event a refund is needed planner will refund client in thirty business days. The refund will be in the form of a Cashier's Check.

6.   Confidential Information

Definition of "Confidential Information" means the terms or conditions of this agreement and any other confidential proprietary information, including information relating to the financial or personal matters relating to either party, identified by the disclosing party as its Confidential Information, whether in oral, written, graphic, or electronic form.

7.   Disclaimer

Lili's Concept is not liable for the security of the event, damages, or any losses that may occur. Lili's Concept will make referrals, but the final selection of vendors are up to the client. Lili's Concept is not to be held liable for any actions, or nonperformance of any vendors, or their parties. If legal intercession is necessary planner will try to work things out with

SAMPLE CONTRACT

client/vendor. If the problem is still not solved the next step will be a local mediation, and then court.

8. Payments to Third-Party Vendors

I, Client, _____ authorize or _____ do not authorize Lili's Concept to make payments to selected vendors on my behalf. By checking and initialing the client agrees to provide Lili's Concept with necessary funding or credit card information to perform these services on my behalf. Lili's Concept will provide a detailed audit of every transaction performed on client's behalf, including date, amount, vendor, and reason for transaction. Verbal consent will be documented in the detailed audit and may be accompanied by phone conversation, which I agree may be recorded by Lili's Concept at any time.

9. General Terms

This Agreement is the exclusive agreement between the parties with respect to the consulting arrangement between the parties. Any modification to this Agreement must be in writing and signed by both parties. This Agreement shall be governed by and construed and enforced in accordance with the laws of the Commonwealth of Virginia. This Agreement may not be assigned by either party without the prior consent of the other party, except that Lili's Concept may hire subcontractors to work with Lili's Concept in performing the Services as long as Lili's Concept has a written nondisclosure agreement with the subcontractor with respect to the Services.

10. Testimonials and Photos

If Client has been pleased with the services received by Lili's Concept, client agrees Lili's Concept may publish their words on its Web site and company literature, and may publish any photos that Lili's Concept or amateur photographer has taken at the event referenced hereof. Client agrees to secure permission from the professional photographer used on the wedding or event day, if any photos taken by a professional photographer are given to Lili's Concept for use in literature, and will not provide any photography to Lili's Concept unless this permission has been secured. Lili's Concept is not responsible for copyright infringement on any of its promotional materials, including company literature and its Web site, if the Client has provided photos for use by Lilli's Concept without securing permission from the professional photographer used on the wedding or event day.

SAMPLE CONTRACT

IN WITNESS WHEREOF, the parties have executed this Service Agreement as of the date first above written.

Lili's Concept

By: _____

Client:

Print Name: _____

Signature: _____

Rights of the Parties

The contract should state what each party's rights are. If there is a breach of contract either party can choose to take the matter to small claims court or in front of a magistrate. A notice such as this might also be sent:

NOTICE OF BREACH OF CONTRACT

Date: _____, 20 _____

To: _____   RE: Breach of Contract

Dear _____

This notice is in reference to the following described contract:

Please be advised that as of _____, 20 _____, we are holding you in BREACH OF CONTRACT for the following reasons:

If this breach of contract is not corrected within _____ days of this notice, we will take further action to protect our rights, which may include the right to obtain a substitute service and charge you for any additional costs. This notice is made under the Uniform Commercial Code and any other applicable laws. All of our rights are reserved under this notice.

_____   _____
Signature   Printed Name

If there is any modification of the contract there needs to be consent by both parties. Either a new contract should be created, or modifications can be documented with each party's signature or initials that they agree to the modification. You can consider using a form such as this:

MODIFICATION OF CONTRACT

Modification of Contract

This Modification of Contract is made on _____, 20 _____, between _____, address: _____, and _____, address: _____ _____

For valuable consideration, the parties agree as follows:

1. The following described contract is attached to this Modification and is made a part of this Modification:

_____
_____
_____

2. The parties agree to modify this contract as follows:

_____
_____
_____

3. All other terms and conditions of the original contract remain in effect without modification.

This Modification binds and benefits both parties and any successors. This document, including the attached contract, is the entire agreement between the parties.

The parties have signed this Modification on the date specified at the beginning of this Modification of Contract.

_____   _____
Signature   Signature

_____   _____
Printed Name   Printed Name

Services Provided to Client

Be clear what services you are providing the client. It should be itemized. Each service should have a time of delivery and when payment is expected. Make sure your client is clear before signing the contract. Make sure each of you have a copy and that they are *notarized*. This will help with any dispute later. If you fail to deliver what you promise, it is better to talk to the client immediately so that something can be worked out and any modifications can be made right away. If you wait until the last minute, you not only open yourself up to a lawsuit, but you risk your reputation.

Marketing

Chapter 7

When you begin to think about marketing your wedding consulting business, start with a wide view. Think about why you decided to form the business in the first place. What does your business have to offer a bride that is unique and different from other consultants? Review your business statement and look specifically at your mission and values statements. Make sure that the description you form about your company is as clear and concise as possible. Your description should answer the following questions:

1. Why is your consulting business going to be a profitable venture?

2. What makes you sure that you will succeed?

3. What do your current or past customers say about your business and its potential?

4. Have you talked with competitors?

5. Will your business be based upon quantity or quality? At what point will you be making a profit or breaking even?

6. If you have not already done so, when do you plan to open your doors for business?

7. Is the consulting business seasonal in nature? Are there times of the year in which you will have more weddings? How will weather affect your business?

8. What will you set as your hours of business? Will you be able to be reached at night? On weekends? Will you be working a flexible schedule?

9. Will you be working at home or will you have an office? Will the location affect your business?

10. Are you working with vendors? How will you contract professionals to work with you?

The next thing you need to do after you have a good description of your business structure is to create a good description of the wedding consulting services that you will be offering. These descriptions should be lively and attract attention. A person should be able to get a clear mental image of your services by reading these descriptions. This will be important when these descriptions are included in marketing and advertising materials. If you plan to have people invest in your business, it is easier for them to make a decision when they have a clear image of the services you will be offering. When creating your descriptions make sure that the language is easy to read, free of jargon, and that the average person reading it will understand and grasp it quickly. Your descriptions should answer the following questions:

1. What services do you offer? These should be broken down individually with a complete description of each. If you have different packages that you are going to offer break them down individually as well.

2. What does your service offer a bride and her family? (i.e. peace of mind, more time)

3. What need does your consulting business fill? (i.e. no consultants in the area, venue needs a full-time consultant)

4. Who are your customers? (This goes back to your demographics)

5. How will the customer benefit from using your consulting service?

6. What makes your wedding consulting business different from your competition's?

7. What are the advantages and disadvantages of your service? (i.e. you are working from home, you live far away from venue sites, or there are not many vendors to choose from)

8. What are the strengths/weaknesses of the services you will offer? (i.e. prices, size of package, your experience)

9. What will be the unique selling point you will use with potential clients? (i.e. a catchy slogan, press releases, awards you have won)

The next item you will need to develop is a business history and your personal experience. This information will be seen by potential clients. It should be produced to impress. When a potential client reads it, it should knock her off her feet and make her want to hire you immediately. This is where you need to shine. Bragging and boasting, as long as it is well founded and honest, is encouraged.

You need to create a narrative about your business. It is the story about when, how, and why your business was born. This should be like telling an epic story, full of drama and excitement.

Here are two examples:

"One day while I was watching a television show about weddings, I thought to myself, 'Wow, I can do that!' So I borrowed some money from my mama and here I am."

"I had a vision. In that vision, I saw a little girl playing in front of a mirror, pretending to be a princess. She had dress-up clothes, makeup, and play jewelry. She spun around and around, imagining what it would be like to dance at her fairy-tale wedding. XYZ Wedding Consultants was created to make that little girl's fantasy come true when she grows up."

Of course, the second paints a picture that a potential bride can relate to. It creates an image of a business that was created for little princesses. Here are some items to think about as you create the written history of your business:

You should include what the current status is of your consulting business. This should state whether you are actively engaged in business or you are just starting out. You will be updating your company history to make it current; every six months to a year is a good schedule to do this. This can be more often if there are exciting additions or changes in your business such as a famous client or an award your business may have received.

You should include what type of business you have, such as a partnership, an LLC, or a sole proprietorship. This gives the reader an idea of who they are dealing with. If you have made any changes to this over time you should state why.

If there have been any changes in management or structure such as adding employees, this should be included in your company history description.

Your narrative should give a list of any milestones and setbacks your company may have experienced, such as moving to an office or losing a partner. This should be a description of how this has affected your business and how it has helped you grow or change your focus.

Once you have completed your company history, you should include your biography and that of any other significant person involved in the company. Here are some dos and don'ts when creating this kind of biography:

Do include your education, job history — make sure it is relevant to wedding consulting — and any experience that makes you the perfect fit for a potential client. Do include who you worked for, how many events you have created, and any famous or influential people you have worked for. Yes, you need to drop names.

Do not exaggerate, make up past clients, or be dishonest in any way. Do not include any irrelevant information such as hosting a mock wedding in the fourth grade.

You want to shine and be noticed. Make every effort to impress and be the star that you are.

Setting Up Your Web Site

One of the largest expenses that many wedding consultants report having to pay for is setting up a Web site. There are many types of Web sites that you could build for your business. Since wedding consulting is service oriented, it should contain facts about your business, your packages, your prices, and how to contact you. You may even consider having a link to send you an e-mail for more information.

Within your site, you can have galleries displaying other weddings you have planned and executed. This can be a great advertising tool. Your Web site can look very much like an online version of your brochure.

You can buy programs such as FrontPage to help you build one. This can be an easy task or difficult. There are many books available that can help you build a simple Web site.

The next question is where to build your site. There are many different options. There are places to place your Web site for free. Look at **http://www.free-webhosts.com** for a list of sites. The problem with this type of Web host is that they can be filled with advertisements that will be placed on your site or will have pop-up ads attached. This is a good option to start out with if you have a limited budget.

There are pay sites where you must pay a monthly or yearly price for hosting your Web site. There are large ones such as **www.yahoo.com** and many other lesser-known ones. Do your research. Some will allow you to use your own domain name. Some of them require that you use their Web site as part of your Web address.

Some of these Web hosting services have simple programs to help you develop your site either offline or online and will give you instructions on how to place your Web pages online.

Driving Business to Your Web Site

You can have another site refer to your site. Another good way to drive people to your site is to make sure the Web site is on your brochures, newsletters, and business cards.

You can write simple articles online and have a link to your Web site. There are many different article-posting sites. When people read your article, say, on how to make bows, they will be directed to visit your Web site.

Mass e-mails that are sent out to advertise your site should have your Web site linked within the text so that if people are interested in your services they can read about them at their leisure.

Join different groups and message boards relating to weddings and join in the discussion. You can then direct people to your site.

Importance of a Home Page

It is the first thing that people see when they come to your Web page. They say first impressions are everything. This is especially true when it comes to your home page. It should be pleasing to the eye and easily direct the user to the different areas on your site such as galleries, pricing, your bio, and any other separate pages you have chosen. If it is hard to navigate or hard to see, then you will lose people's interest and possibly lose a potential sale. Keep it simple. Also, do not put a lot of graphics on your home page as this can slow down the time it takes to load and people may not wait for it to load.

Becoming Google Friendly

There are two main ways services such as Google will pick up your page. The first is that you pay a fee to have your Web site displayed when certain key words are entered in a search. This can be rather costly.

The other way is to make your Web site search-engine optimized. This has to do with the way words are displayed on your Web pages. You should have certain keywords and phrases on your pages in order for a search engine to choose your Web site to display. This can take a lot of work and an understanding of the Web. There are professionals that are experts in optimizing your Web site. They can be expensive, but they will make sure that your site is picked up on Google and other search engines more often.

If you choose to try to optimize your site yourself, there are many sites that can help you, such as **www.scrubtheweb.com**. There are also programs that you can buy such as WebPosition Gold that will help you optimize your site.

Should I Do It Myself or Hire Someone?

Are you computer-savvy enough to create an eye-popping Web site? Most wedding consultants have many other things to worry about besides sitting in front of a computer and using programs that may not be familiar. That is not to say a good Web site is not important; it is just that it can be very time consuming. When you read the case studies you will see that other wedding consultants spent a good deal of their start-up money on having someone else develop a Web site for them. They say it was money well spent.

If you have the skills and the time, then you can save yourself a chunk of money. Something to consider is what happens when your business grows. What is your plan to have your Web site grow with it? Some Web designers have packages in which they will do updates for you for a fee.

Business Cards

Do yourself a favor and spend the money to buy good stationery and business cards. Do not waste your time printing them out on a printer. Nothing screams cheap and unprofessional like having homemade business cards.

That does not mean you have to spend a fortune having business cards made. You can have 100 cards printed for about $10. Have them printed on good, heavy, stock paper. You are trying to win people over with your style and panache. It begins with your business card.

Having good stationery is important. You will be sending out thank-you cards and letters to vendors and clients quite often. Having stationery made of good stock paper with your logo and contact information is classy.

Your business card should have the logo and business name prominently displayed. The contact information and your name should be in smaller type. Pick a color that is easy on the eyes. If you choose a background, make it simple. The more things you put on a card the harder it will be to read. Remember KISS!

Chapter 8

Standard Operating Procedures

One way to streamline what you do is to create a manual of your Standard Operating Procedures (SOP). This manual will have a lot of helpful information for you to use in case you forget how to get a license for serving liquor at an event. This manual will be invaluable to those working for you and volunteering. It will spell out in detail how things are supposed to be done and to what standard they should be completed. It can act as a training manual for employees. This manual can help save you time and aggravation at a later date. Keep it handy along with your emergency kit.

Evaluating Your Success After Six Months

One way to evaluate how your business is doing and ways to improve it is what is called a SWOT analysis. SWOT stands for strengths, weaknesses, opportunities, and threats.

The strengths and weaknesses are determined in reference to your competition and others in the industry, not based upon your own history. Strengths and weaknesses are internal to your consulting business. Opportunities and threats are from external sources such as your competition. These competitors should be current and new arrivals upon the wedding consulting scene.

Using a SWOT analysis will help you focus your energy on areas where you are the strongest and concentrating on where the greatest opportunities are.

How to Do a SWOT Analysis

The first thing you will consider is your business strengths. Included here is a worksheet, which can also be found on the CD. Here are some things to consider as you fill out this worksheet:

What sets your service apart in the industry?

What does your business do well?

What resources and vendors do you have to work with?

What do your clients say your company's strengths are? You can get this information from sending them an evaluation of your service — see the next section for examples.

When you fill your worksheet out make sure you are honest, and do not be modest. Put items in that make your company shine.

SWOT Worksheet — Strengths

On this worksheet, make sure you are adding your company's internal strengths and what sets them apart from other wedding consulting businesses both old and new. You can add as many strengths as you wish. When you are done figure out what your top eight strengths are.

STRENGTHS

Your Company's Strengths:

1. _____
2. _____
3. _____

Description of the Strengths (Be Clear and Concise):

1. _____
_____
_____

2. _____
_____
_____

3. _____
_____
_____

Ways to Continue to Build on the Strengths:

1. _____
_____
_____

2. _____
_____
_____

3. _____
_____
_____

The next thing you will evaluate is your company's weaknesses. As you fill out the weaknesses here are some questions to help you through the process:

- What are things that can improve in your business?

- What does your business not do as well as you would like?

💜   What things have your clients said need improvement in your company? (Again, this can be drawn from comments or a survey done with them after you have completed your service with them.)

💜   Is your competition doing better than you are?

Just like the strengths, you want to be honest. No one needs to see this list except you, so put it all out there.

SWOT Worksheet—Weaknesses

On this worksheet you are going to list the weaknesses of your wedding consulting business. These can be deficiencies in the area of resources or capabilities of your company. These are items that do not enable you to follow your mission and values statements during the course of doing business. You may add as many weaknesses as you wish. When you are done figure out what your eight highest-priority weaknesses are.

WEAKNESSES
Your Company's Weaknesses
1. _____
2. _____
3. _____
Description of the Weaknesses (Be Clear and Concise):
1. _____
2. _____
3. _____

WEAKNESSES
Ways to Continue to Build on the Weaknesses:
1. _____
_____
_____
2. _____
_____
_____
3. _____
_____
_____

As described earlier, opportunities are from external sources. As you fill out your opportunities worksheet consider using the following questions:

♥ Where are the best opportunities for your company?

♥ What are the new trends in the wedding consulting industry?

♥ Where can you find these new trends?

♥ Are there changes in the market that can improve your business?

♥ Are there new vendors or venues to be considered?

♥ Are there new bridal shows or places you can find new clients?

You can look at your strengths list and consider what and where are the opportunities that can help you bolster your strengths. You can also look at your weaknesses list and consider where you might find ways to eliminate some of these weaknesses.

SWOT Worksheet — Opportunities

On this worksheet you are considering outside factors and people that can improve and help your wedding consulting company. You can list as many opportunities on your sheet as you wish. When you are done, compare them to your vision statement, values statement, and any other component in your business plan. See if they resonate with one another. You may have to adjust your plan or your opportunity to make sure you are placing your focus on the right items. When you have completed your changes, come up with a plan to implement utilizing your opportunities.

OPPORTUNITIES
Your Company's Opportunities:
1. _____
2. _____
3. _____
Description of the Opportunities (Be Clear and Concise):
1. _____
2. _____
3. _____
Ways to Continue to Build on the Opportunities:
1. _____
2. _____

OPPORTUNITIES
3. _____
_____
_____

The last component of your SWOT analysis is threats. These are external threats and should not be confused with weaknesses. Here are some questions to help you fill out your threat worksheet:

♥   What obstacles does your business face?

♥   What is your competition doing that is affecting your company?

♥   Are there any regulations or laws that have changed about operating a wedding consulting business?

♥   Is your company facing financial and debt problems?

SWOT Worksheet — Threats

On this worksheet, you will be listing situations, people, and factors that affect your wedding consulting business in a negative way. You may list as many factors as you wish. Decide which factors are in your control and which ones are not. Come up with a plan to try to reduce or eliminate threats that you do have control over.

THREATS
Your Company's Threats:
1. _____
2. _____
3. _____

THREATS

Description of the Threats (Be Clear and Concise):

1. _____
   _____
   _____

2. _____
   _____
   _____

3. _____
   _____
   _____

Ways to Continue to Build on the Threats:

1. _____
   _____
   _____

2. _____
   _____
   _____

3. _____
   _____
   _____

Surveys

When you have completed work with a client, it is always nice to send them a thank-you card. In it, you can add two important things to help your company. The first is some extra business cards and the other is a short survey.

On the back of the business card write the name of your client. That way when a new potential client calls, you will know where the referral came from and whether your word-of-mouth business is successful. Keep a running tally of the number of word-of-mouth referrals you get. It can help your SWOT analysis as well as your marketing strategy.

The survey should be brief. It is good if you can write it on self-mailing cards so that when they are done all they have to do is send it back in the mail with the postage already paid. Keep a tally of the number of returned surveys to see whether this is a good marketing strategy for you.

SAMPLE THANK-YOU LETTER

XYZ Wedding Consultants
123 Main Street
Anywhere, USA

January 18, 2008
Mrs. Newly Wed
456 N. Main Street
Anywhere, USA

Dear Mrs. Wed:

On behalf of everyone at XYZ Wedding Consultants, thank you for choosing us to make your wedding day dream a reality.

We are committed to providing brides, grooms, and their family and friends the highest level of customer satisfaction possible. If for any reason you have questions or comments, we are delighted to hear from you. Call us at 1-800-555-1234, or send us an e-mail at XYZweddingconsultants@service.com. You can expect us to respond to your e-mail within 24 hours.

Our company relies on the generosity of you, our clients, in spreading the word about our superb wedding consulting services. I have included some business cards that I hope you will give to your family and friends so that we can make their wedding day as special and stress-free as the one we provided for you.

In addition, I have included a quick survey. It takes less than five minutes to fill out and you can fold it and send it back to me, as it is a self-addressed stamped postcard. Please be honest and add any comments that we can use to improve the way we do business. If you would like to add positive comments, we would love to use them on our Web site and promotional materials.

Again, thank you for your patronage. We wish you the best of luck in your new life.

Sincerely,

Loreena Brown

Wedding Consultant

SAMPLE SURVEY

XYZ Wedding Consultants Survey

Please fill out the following survey. Circle the number that most closely represents your answer: 1 is strongly agree, 2 is agree, 3 is no opinion, 4 disagree, and 5 is strongly disagree. When you are finished, please fold this paper in half with the address label and stamp on the outside, and mail it back to us. You can staple or tape the ends firmly. Thank you for your time and generosity.

1. Loreena Brown paid attention to every detail.

   1...2...3...4...5

2. Loreena listened to my vision of the wedding.

   1...2...3...4...5

3. Loreena was always able to be reached.

   1...2...3...4...5

4. I will recommend Loreena to friends and family for their weddings.

   1...2...3...4...5

5. Loreena worked within my budget.

   1...2...3...4...5

6. Loreena was knowledgeable about wedding trends.

   1...2...3...4...5

7. Loreena is someone I trust.

   1...2...3...4...5

8. Loreena was able to coordinate vendors at a fair price.

   1...2...3...4...5

9. Loreena was able to secure the venue I wanted.

   1...2...3...4...5

10. Loreena was sensitive to my feelings and my family's feelings.

    1...2...3...4...5

How to Look at Success After One Year

When you reach the one-year mark it is time look at where you have been, where you are, and where you want to go. If you did not already do a SWOT analysis or want to do another one, this is a good time to do so.

In addition, you should send out surveys to your vendors. These are similar to the ones you would send to clients. This provides feedback about strengths and weaknesses of your company.

It is at the one-year mark that you have to do some honest soul searching. Does your wedding consulting business have what it takes to succeed?

This does not depend on the money you are making. It is a mistake to use this as the one component to determine whether your business is viable or not. It can take a few years to get any small business to make a profit. You do want to at least break even. You may be worrying about how to keep the lights on at home. You may need to work a part-time job until your business can turn a profit.

If you are getting a steady stream of referrals and your calendar is beginning to fill up, then this is a greater indication of success. There are some things to consider when looking at work as a wedding consultant. There are times of the year when more brides get married, so you should plan time off during the slower periods. June is a big month. This is followed by August, July, September, October, May, April, November, December, March, February, and January. This will be different from area to area, based upon climate, cultural influences, current trends, and availability issues. You should keep a calendar from a past year and look at when the most weddings were as your own guide. They can change slightly from year to year but you should find that they follow a predictable pattern.

Comparing Costs to Profits at the One-, Three-, and Five-Year Marks

In order to look at your profits after one, three, and five years, you must have kept immaculate records. Let us pull some graphs and figures from your business plan to help assess what you should be looking at to be able to compare costs to profits.

Break-Even Analysis

The following table and chart summarize our break-even analysis. This is what you have to make compared to what your costs are. If you are not making this at the three- and five-year mark, first you are not making any profit, and second, you may need to change the way you do business or find some other type of business. One of the easiest ways to tip the scales here is to raise your prices. If you are at the three- or five-year mark then you have gained experience and you should raise your prices. In the usual economy the cost of everything goes up every year and so it will be harder to make the break-even point if you do not raise your prices.

The great news is, unless your bride is unlucky, you will not have repeat business. You do not have to explain to anyone why your prices have gone up unless there is a situation in which someone knows how much you charged their friend or family member. You can have a couple of different responses, both of which are honest. The first is that their wedding is different and that you treat each bride and each wedding separately. The second response is straight to the point, the cost of doing business has become more expensive and so you had to raise your prices just to break even.

Monthly Revenue Break-Even	$5,468
Assumptions:	
Average Percent Variable Cost:	0%
Estimated Monthly Fixed Cost	$5,468

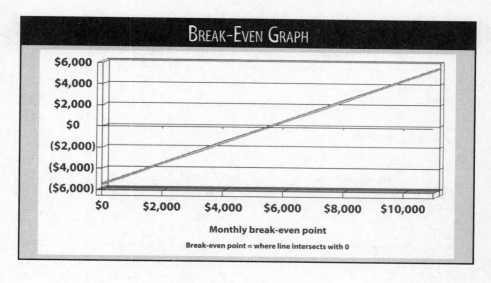

An example of projected profit and loss is shown in the following table. This table looks at what you are making in sales and what the cost of doing business is. When the amount is below the break-even point, you are having a loss. When you are above the break-even point, you are making a profit. The net profit is the actual amount of profit you are making.

PRO FORMA PROFIT AND LOSS STATEMENT			
	2007	2008	2009
Sales	$95,300	$114,360	$125,796
Direct Cost of Sales	$0	$0	$0
Other	$0	$0	$0
Total Cost of Sales	$0	$0	$0
Gross Margin	$95,300	$114,360	$125,796
Gross Margin %	100.00%	100.00%	100.00%
Expenses			
Payroll	$53,100	$76,200	$85,800
Sales and Marketing and Other Expenses	$4,550	$1,000	$2,000
Depreciation	$0	$0	$0
Leased Equipment	$0	$0	$0

Projected Profit and Loss

Pro Forma Profit and Loss Statement			
	2007	2008	2009
Utilities	$0	$0	$0
Insurance	$0	$0	$0
Rent	$0	$0	$0
Payroll Taxes	$7,965	$11,430	$12,870
Other	$0	$0	$0
Total Operating Expenses	**$65,615**	**$88,630**	**$100,670**
Profit Before Interest	$29,685	$25,730	$25,126
Taxable Amount	$29,685	$25,730	$25,126
Interest Expense	$0	$0	$0
Taxes Incurred	$7,421	$6,433	$6,386
Net Profit	**$22,264**	**$19,297**	**$18,740**
Net Profit/Sales	**23.36%**	**16.87%**	**14.90%**

Profit Monthly

You can look at and chart your monthly profits if you do not want to wait a year. In addition, you can look at which months you are making the most money and when you are not making as much. The months where profits are lower, you can concentrate on other aspects of your business, such as marketing, or you can do different kinds of events and expand your wedding consulting business into event planning.

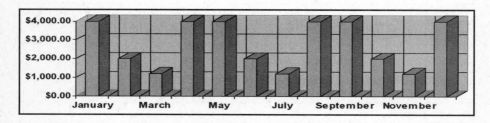

Profit Yearly

You can use these charts to look at your business at the three-year mark or even expand this into a five-year mark. Hopefully you should see your profits rise over three to five years. It helps you predict what the following year's profits should be.

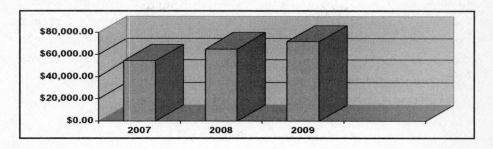

Gross Margin Monthly

Gross margin is the amount of contribution to your business after you have paid for fixed and variable costs, and what amount is needed to cover overhead. What does this mean? Well, suppose it costs you a certain amount to provide your wedding consulting service such as the cost of phone calls, travel expenses, or the cost of materials needed to set up and decorate. This is important because if you charge $1,500 and you spent $700 in materials and expenses then your gross margin would be $800. You would need to increase your price to cover your costs so that you will know exactly what you are making. Here are some equations to help you determine your gross margin. The first helps you determine exactly how much money you are making when you charge a price. Revenue is what your are charging for your service.

$$\text{Gross Margin} = \text{Revenue} - \text{Cost of Doing a Wedding}$$
$$\$800 = \$1500 - \$700$$

To calculate your gross margin in terms of percentage you would use the following equation. This is important to see the percentage of what you are charging and what you are actually making. You do not want to be charging too little and not making enough money.

$$\text{Gross margin percentage} = (\text{Revenue} - \text{Cost of Doing a Wedding}) / \text{Revenue} \times 100$$
$$53\% = (1500 - 700) / 1500 \times 100$$

So if you are doing weddings for $1500 you are really doing it at a 53 percent gross margin. How can you use this information? When calculating how much to charge your clients you can use the percentage to come up with a price that is fair and still makes you money. In this case you will choose a percentage that you wish to make. In our example let us say you want to make a 50% gross margin. In our example in 2007 it has been costing you $800. You will use the following formula to calculate your price:

> Your price = cost/(1 – GM%)
> Your price =800/(1 – 0.5)=800/0.5 = $1600

Now suppose in 2009 it costs $900. What does your price need to be with this new increase?

> Your price = 900/(1 – 0.5)=900/0.5 = $1800

That is a $200 increase in what you charge. This is a good way to calculate price. You can do this with every contract as long as you know how much you want to make on every wedding. Keep track of these numbers when you are reviewing your business at the one-, three-, and five-year mark. As you gain reputation and experience you can raise your margin incrementally.

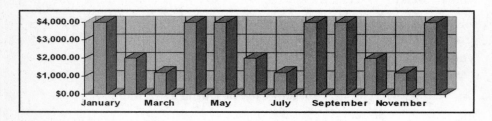

Gross Margin Yearly

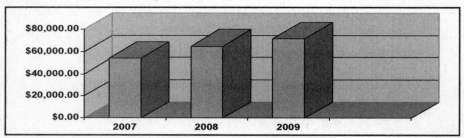

Projected Cash Flow

The following chart and table show cash flow projections. The term cash flow refers to the amount of cash being received and spent by a business during a defined period of time. This information can be used to evaluate the state of performance of your business. A business can be profitable but have problems with a cash flow and even have a shortage of available cash. Money can be tied up in other areas. Cash flow can help evaluate your company's growth and viability.

Cash Flow

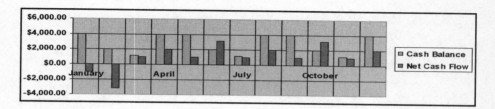

PRO FORMA CASH FLOW			
	2001	2002	2003
Cash received			
Cash received from operations			
Cash sales	$38,120	$45,744	$50,318
Cash from receivables	$45,494	$66,279	$74,075
Subtotal cash from operations	$83,614	$112,023	$124,393
Additional cash received			
Sales Tax, VAT, HST/GST, received	$0	$0	$0
New current borrowing	$0	$0	$0
New other liabilities (interest-free)	$0	$0	$0
New long-term liabilities	$0	$0	$0
Sales of other current assets	$0	$0	$0
Sales of long-term assets	$0	$0	$0
New investment received	$0	$0	$0
Subtotal cash received	**$83,614**	**$112,023**	**$124,393**

Pro Forma Cash Flow			
	2001	2002	2003
Expenditures			
Expenditures from operations			
Cash spending	$53,100	$76,200	$85,800
Still payments	$18,072	$19,177	$21,059
Subtotal spent on operations	$71,172	$95,377	$106,859
Additional cash spent			
Sales tax, VAT, HST/GST paid out	$0	$0	$0
Principal repayment of current borrowing	$0	$0	$0
Other liabilities' principal repayment	$0	$0	$0
Long-term liabilities' principal repayment	$0	$0	$0
Purchase other current assets	$0	$0	$0
Purchase long-term assets	$0	$0	$0
Dividends	$0	$0	$0
Subtotal cash spent	$71,172	$95,377	$106,859
Net cash flow	**$12,442**	**$16,646**	**$17,534**
Cash balance	**$17,442**	**$34,088**	**$51,623**

Travel Costs for In-Person Events

When trying to calculate the cost of your services, you must calculate your traveling costs. You can put this into your contract two different ways. One is that you include a set amount in your fee to cover traveling costs. This works best when you have been doing weddings for a while and you know how much traveling you will be doing for a particular type of event or a particular venue.

Another way is to add to the contract that the bride will pay you mileage and you will keep track of how many miles you go during the planning and execution of her wedding. If you are working two weddings and are going to a florist to conduct business for both weddings, then you can split the cost between the two clients for that trip.

Whichever way you choose, make sure you are clear with your client and that it is stated clearly on the contract. There may be other items such as copying or material for decorating that may be beyond the regular cost of the package. Make sure you let the client know when this occurs and make sure you state in the contract that they can be charged for things not included in the package they have chosen.

Scheduling

Your calendar must become your best friend. It must go and be everywhere you are. Whether it is a paper or electronic version, you must be able to lay your hands on it day or night. You could bump into someone at a movie theater and they may mention they are getting married on a certain date and they are wondering whether you can help. Having a calendar can be a lifesaver, because you do not want to put them off any more than you want to overcommit yourself.

Some consultants make a copy of their schedule once a week. That way if it is lost, not everything will be lost. This may seem extreme for some consultants, but if you ever lose your calendar, you will wish you had done this.

When you schedule your day and events, schedule smartly. Do not overbook or overcommit yourself. You will end up burning out and the quality of your work will suffer. You need your wits and patience and if you are overworked then these important attributes will be affected. This is not good business.

Schedule in times to take care of yourself. You are in the helping field. You offer so much time, emotional support, and essentially your soul to do what you do. So you need to take care of yourself. In the first year or two it may be hard to schedule a vacation, but once things are moving, decide on some days to take off and stick with them. You are the boss, so be kind your employee — you.

To save time and money, try to schedule your day in such a way that you are going places that are close together. You can waste a lot of precious time running back and forth.

Unless you are experienced, you should not overlap too many weddings. Do not book two or three weddings in one weekend. It will be tempting because it could mean more revenue, but it is an equation for disaster. You never know what can happen in a wedding, and so if it takes more time to deal with an emergency, it can have a domino effect on the rest of your commitments. If you are at the point of having more weddings than you can handle, it may be time to consider hiring help or taking on a partner who can balance the workload.

Hired Help

If you decide to hire employees, there are taxes and expenses to be considered. If your business grows to the point where you feel stretched and you have determined that your business is viable and is making a profit, then you can consider hiring on employees. You may need to check with the laws concerning hiring in your area and state. Make sure you follow the guidelines of fair hiring practices. A good place to look for and request copies of this information is from the United States Office of Personnel Management. They have the current laws and practices of hiring and maintaining employees. They can be found at **www.opm.gov**.

How can you be sure you are hiring the right person? You could hire an intern. These can be energetic, motivated college students that may be studying small business. They will want to help in addition to making a little money doing it. Check with your local colleges, community colleges, and business schools.

Take your time. The person you hire must be someone you trust, because you will probably hire them to work independently, doing tasks that you would normally be doing. They need to do them in such a way that you can feel confident they can do it according to the same standards to which you would do them.

Here are a few areas in which you may decide to hire personnel to help you in your wedding consulting business:

♥ If you have an office with a few employees you might consider an office manager. They can take care of day-to-day administrative, clerical, and office supply duties.

♥ As you grow you may need another wedding planner. This person should have experience in wedding planning, and be dedicated to your business. Be sure to check a number of references closely before hiring this person as they could help or destroy your businesses name and reputation.

♥ If you need some help at the venue site or in creating ideas for certain weddings, you might consider hiring a part-time or full-time designer. This person should be creative, flexible, and have great artistic skills.

♥ If you are running a large company, you may need to hire a public relations (PR) person to take care of talking to clients, vendors, or the general public. They must be diplomatic, have communication skills, and be able to answer questions under pressure.

♥ If you just do not have the time to market your company you can hire a freelance, part-time, or full-time marketing manager. They can take care of advertising, promotion, analyzing the market, and steering your company in the right direction.

♥ If you just want to hand over the financial aspects of your business to someone that has a love for numbers then you may consider hiring a bookkeeper. This should be someone with some education and experience. Sometimes a retired bookkeeper that is looking for some part-time work may be your best option.

♥ If you like making a mess, but not cleaning it up, you may consider hiring a venue assistant. This person helps make sure everything is set up and then coordinates or actually does the tearing down after a wedding event on site.

♥ If you would like someone to help greet family and friends at a wedding along with running concessions, collecting presents, and coordinating volunteers, then you should consider hiring a house staff person. This person should be good at directing people, answering questions, and should be trusted — or even better, bonded — with regard to money.

♥ If you want to help create invitations, crafts, and other decorations, you might consider hiring an arts and crafts person. A person that can do calligraphy is a valuable asset.

♥ If you want to get into the vendor side of things, you may want to hire kitchen staff, or a bartender, as well as servers, dishwashers, and someone to supervise them. This is a big undertaking as you would need to set up a kitchen or get a bartending license. It can improve your profits, but it can entail a lot more work.

♥ If you need someone to move supplies to venues, you may want to hire someone to be a delivery person. They can just work on the days of weddings as contract labor or you can have them doing other duties on the days you need an extra hand.

♥ A notary can be a lifesaver in your line of work — from signing contracts to notarizing wedding certificates, they can be invaluable. You may consider becoming a notary yourself as well.

These are just some of the people you may want or need to hire. Some of these jobs can be combined, as one job may not offer enough hours for someone to commit to working for you. Once you have decided to hire the person you may want them to sign a contract. This is in addition to having them filling out W-4 and state tax forms.

GENERAL EMPLOYMENT CONTRACT

This Contract is made on _____ , 20 ____ , between _____
_____ ,Employer, of _____ , City of _____
__, State of_____ , and _____ , Employee, of _____
_____ City of _____ , State of _____ .

GENERAL EMPLOYMENT CONTRACT

In order for both parties to work together as a team, the Employer and Employee agree as follows:

1.　　The Employee agrees to perform the following duties and job description: (write down every aspect of the job the person is to do. If you add items later, it should be added on this form and initialed or a new form should be created.)

This is considered a full/part-time position.

2.　　The Employee will begin work on _____, 20 ____. This position shall continue for a period of _____. (Either a time frame or until a specific date.)

3.　　The Employee will be paid the following:
Weekly salary: (this may be hourly, monthly, or per event)
The Employee will also be given the following benefits: (This may not be applicable, but make sure that you follow state and federal guidelines concerning benefits.)

　　　Sick Pay:

　　　Vacations:

　　　Bonuses:

　　　Retirement Benefits:

　　　Insurance Benefits:

4.　　The Employee agrees to abide by all rules and regulations of the Employer at all times while employed. In addition, they will read and agree to the company's business plan, vision statement, and value statement.

5.　　This Contract may be terminated by:
(a) Breach of this Contract by the Employee;
(b) The expiration of this Contract without renewal;
(c) Death of the employee;
(d) Incapacitation of the Employee for over _____ days in any one year.
(You may choose to add, delete, or modify anything you choose in this section.)

6.　　The Employee agrees to sign the following additional documents as a condition to obtaining employment: (You can add other documents such

GENERAL EMPLOYMENT CONTRACT

as a noncompete agreement and an agreement not to divulge anything about the company and how it operates to any outside entity.)

7. Any dispute between the Employer and Employee related to this Contract will be settled by voluntary mediation. If mediation is unsuccessful, the dispute will be settled by binding arbitration using an arbitrator of the American Arbitration Association. (This is professional organization that can help settle disputes outside of court for a fee. More information can be found at **http://www.adr.org**.)

8. Any additional terms of this Contract:

9. No modification of this Contract will be effective unless it is in writing and is signed by both the Employer and Employee. This Contract binds and benefits both parties and any successors. Time is of the essence of this Contract. This document is the entire agreement between the parties. This Contract is governed by the laws of the State of _____

Dated: _____

_____
Signature of Employer

_____
Printed name of Employer

_____
Signature of Employee

_____
Printed name of Employee

(You may want a notary to sign and seal this agreement.)

You may also want to have a written contract with a particular vendor. You would sign the contract if you are having them subcontract the work. If the client is hiring them directly and will be paying them directly, then the client would sign the contract. It is advisable to always have a signed contract with a vendor. It can save you money, time, and aggravation if you do. If you ever have to take a vendor to court, having a signed contract can be the document to tip the scales in your favor.

VENDOR AGREEMENT

This Agreement is made on _____, 20 ____ , between_____
_____, Company (your wedding consulting business, or you can put the client's name), of _____, City of _____
___, State of _____ and _____, Vendor, of _____, City of _____, State of _____
_____.

1.   The Vendor, as an independent contractor, agrees to furnish all of the labor and materials to do the following portions of the work specified in the Agreement between the Company and the Vendor dated _____
     ____, 20 ____:

2.   The Vendor agrees that the following portions of the total work will be completed by the dates specified:

     Work:

     Dates:

3.   The Vendor agrees to perform this work in a professional manner according to standard practices in their industry. If any plans or specifications are part of this job, they are attached to and are part of this Contract.

4.   The Contractor agrees to pay the Subcontractor as full payment $_____
     _____ for doing the work outlined above. This price will be paid to the Vendor on satisfactory completion of the work in the following manner and on the following dates:

     Work:

     Dates:

5.   The Company and Vendor may agree to extra services and work, but any such extras must be set out and agreed to in writing by both the Company and the Vendor.

6.   The Vendor agrees to indemnify and hold the Contractor harmless from any claims or liability arising from the Vendor's work under this Agreement.

7.   No modification of this Agreement will be effective unless it is in writing and is signed by both parties. This Agreement binds and benefits both parties and any successors. Time is of the essence of this Agreement. This document, including any attachments, is the entire agreement between the parties. This Agreement is governed by the laws of the State of _____
     _____.

VENDOR AGREEMENT

Dated: _____

_____

Signature of Contractor

_____

Name of Contractor

_____

Signature of Subcontractor

_____

Name of Subcontractor

(You may want a notary to sign and seal this agreement.)

The next few sections that are listed here should be a part of your business plan before you begin to hire employees. It helps you and the person you hire know what is going to be expected of them, what the structure of the company is, and what the management structure will be.

Management Summary

This section deals with the structure of your company. You will list what type of company — sole proprietorships, partnership, or other — you have set up. Then detail who the owners are and what the actual management structure is. You can add a chart that illustrates the management system and the order of management, from the employee right up through the owners. This ordering helps people know who they are responsible for, what they are responsible for, and what the chain of command is. This can change over time as positions are added, combined, or removed.

Also in this section you will explain why you need the employees and the overall plan of paying for and supporting certain positions in the company. In addition to listing who the owners and managers are, list their qualifications and education. This justifies the management choices and documents who the experts are in different aspects of the company.

Personnel Plan

In this section, you will have a breakdown of the financial burden of the employees in the company. This includes how and what you plan to pay for yourself. It will also detail what it will take to be able to hire new positions and what the projected cost will be.

PERSONNEL PLAN			
	2007	2008	2009
Owner	$53,100	$76,200	$85,800
Other	$0	$0	$20,000
Total People	0	0	0
Total Payroll	$53,100	$76,200	$105,800

End-of-the-Year Financial Analysis

At the end of the year you will want to assess where your business is going. Earlier in the chapter you looked at costs and an analysis of your situation at the one-, three-, and five-year mark. Here is a worksheet that will allow you to review how you are doing and in what areas you need improvement in order to keep your business salient.

END-OF-THE-YEAR FINANCIAL ASSESSMENT

The current financial status of your company: _____
_____

Income and Expenses

Record what the annual expenses were for the first year in the following categories:

(Fill in the amounts in the following categories if they apply to your company. You should be able to draw these figures from your records over the past year.)

Advertising expenses: _____

Auto expenses: _____

Cleaning and maintenance expenses: _____

Dues and publications: _____

End-of-the-Year Financial Assessment

Office equipment expenses: _____

Business insurance expenses: _____

Legal and accounting expenses: _____

Business meals and lodging: _____

Miscellaneous expenses: _____

Postage expenses: _____

Office rent/mortgage expenses: _____

Repair expenses: _____

Office supplies: _____

Federal unemployment taxes: _____

State unemployment taxes: _____

Telephone/Internet expenses: _____

Utility expenses: _____

Wages and commissions: _____

Record the first year's annual income from the following sources:

Service income:: _____

Miscellaneous income (this can be any tips or bonuses you may have received, or any products you created that are not considered a service, such as bouquets or invitations): _____

Types of Debts

(Fill in all of the types of debts that are applicable to your company. You should draw these amounts from your records.)

Current liabilities: _____

Taxes due: _____

Accounts payable: _____

Short-term loans/notes payable: _____

Payroll accrued: _____

Miscellaneous: _____

END-OF-THE-YEAR FINANCIAL ASSESSMENT

Long-term liabilities: _____

Other loans/notes payable: _____

Financial Needs

Based on the estimated profits and losses of your company, what finances will you need to keep the company going?

Second year: _____

Third year: _____

Fourth year: _____

Fifth year: _____

Estimate the cash flow for the business for the next four years:

Second year: _____

Third year: _____

Fourth year: _____

Fifth year: _____

From what sources are the necessary funds expected to be raised?

Cash on hand: _____

Personal funds: _____

Family: _____

Friends: _____

Conventional bank financing: _____

Finance companies: _____

U.S. Small Business Administration: _____

Record the cost of doing business for the first year:

(This includes traveling, phone bills, or anything else you needed to perform your duties as a wedding consultant. This can be calculated using the gross margin.)

Assets and liabilities _____

What forms of credit have already been used by your company? _____

What is the cash flow of your company? _____

What are the sources of that cash flow? _____

END-OF-THE-YEAR FINANCIAL ASSESSMENT

What types of bank accounts are in place for the business and what are the current balances? _____

What types of assets are currently owned by the business? (Fill in the amounts that are applicable to your company. You should be able to calculate these based upon your records from the past year.)

Current assets: _____

Cash in bank: _____

Cash on hand: _____

Accounts receivable: _____

Autos/trucks: _____

Equipment: _____

Amount of depreciation taken on any of above: _____

Fixed nondepreciable: _____

Miscellaneous: _____

Once you have filled in the worksheet, look closely at the results of your analysis. Do you see any problems? What are the highlights? Are there any obvious cash flow problems? Was your income enough to cover your debts or did you need to use your own personal finances or financial assistance from friends or family?

You should do this analysis every year. The third and fifth years are the breaking points of most wedding consulting businesses. It is at these times that you can clearly assess both financial stability and your continued personal investment into your business.

How to Assess Success

While it is important to look at the financial stability of your business as a milestone of success, there are other facets to consider when discussing the success of your wedding consulting business. Consider these questions:

1.　Do you feel as though you are providing a necessary service to the wedding industry?

2.　Does your target market have enough clients to continue to support your business now and in the future?

3.　Do you have enough financial support to continue to keep your business running for at least three more years?

4.　Do you feel that you have a strong and clear business plan that can help you navigate your business and give you direction should you need help?

5.　Is your support team strong, positive, and available?

6.　Is your number-one priority still to provide the best service and to transform dreams into reality for your clients?

7.　Have you done a good job keeping up with records and paying taxes? Do you have a clear idea how your business is doing financially at any time?

8.　Do you have a clear understanding of your competition, who they are, what they offer, and how they are doing in comparison to your consulting business?

9.　Do you have the tenacity to change when necessary in your business, especially when times become stressful?

10.　Do you still love wedding consulting as a career?

Ongoing Generation of New Clients

The wedding consulting business is all about relationships. It is not what you know, but who you know. Word of mouth can make you or break you. In addition to building great and fabulous relationships with your clients you need to build lasting relationships with your vendors as well.

Having your clients write a letter of recommendation to use on your Web site and marketing materials is brilliant. It creates word of mouth that you can use over and over again, where and when you want to.

One way to get more positive word of mouth is to call a client a few weeks after the event. This is to see how they are doing and if they were satisfied with your service. This could generate referrals immediately. You can use your satisfied client's name as a way to cold call a potential client.

Another way to generate more clients is to do charity events or offer services to brides who would normally not be able to afford your services. Make sure you have a press release to get your name and services mentioned with the charitable act that you have done. People will associate your name with a positive act.

Keeping Productivity on the Upswing

Keeping your business alive takes work. You cannot expect the clients to come and knock on your door and that everything will take care of itself. One of the ways to keep things flowing is to be aware of the costs of doing business and how it controls your profit level. Do you know what the costs of doing business are? Have you sat down and figured out what all of your expenses are? Is the cost of doing business increasing or decreasing?

One of the ways to monitor this is to follow cost trends. The first thing you will need to do is group your business transactions into various categories. Decide where the majority of the costs are in your company. What are your fixed and variable costs of doing business?

In your business plan, you learned how to create and use gross profit margins when coming up with a price to charge clients. You need to adjust your margin along with the ebbs and flows of the industry.

Part of keeping productivity is looking at your market. The number of clients determines your potential profits as well as defining how much of a threat your competition is to your business. If there are too many wedding consultants targeting a small market it can create a situation in which you may not be able to survive.

Is your market growing year to year? A growing market is one of the best indicators that you will have your fair chunk of the market. As the market shrinks, the competition will be greater, but as it grows your market share will grow with it.

Never let up and always keep focused on your goals. You should continue to find ways to increase your market, increase your margin of profit, and reduce your costs. These things do not happen on their own; therefore, you must work hard and be vigilant.

The Psychology Behind Consulting

Chapter 9

Why It Works

People look to experts in many areas of their lives. If they have a clogged drain, they call a plumber; if their car is broken, they look to a mechanic; so it is little surprise when it comes to planning a wedding that brides would look to a wedding consultant. Wedding consultants fill a void that has been created by parents not taking care of all the details as they once did.

In addition, a wedding is a major business undertaking. There are vendors, materials, food, and permits, and coordinating all of these things on top of the stress of working and of being engaged can be overwhelming to a bride.

When someone who is an expert offers a hand to help, a bride will jump on the opportunity to dump the whole mess on someone else's plate.

In addition to being good managers, wedding consultants are artists. They make colors match and create magic through music, lighting, and decorations. They are magicians that can transform a big ugly room into a fairy-tale dream filled with light, color, taste, and sound. People are willing to pay for that level of artistry.

Correlations With Success

So what makes a successful wedding consultant? Balance. They are a mixture of artist, manager, counselor, friend, and planner. They know how to work with people and they know how to run a tight business. It is the in-between times that define whether a wedding consultant will really make it. What they are doing to keep their business rolling and growing will determine if they will survive the first few years.

It is a very rewarding profession. The main event is a happy one filled with good food, good music, smiles, laughter, and some tears, but in the end it is a celebration of life and new beginnings and possibilities. To be in the position to direct that beautiful symphony is an awesome place to be.

Personality Types and Success

Obviously meek people need not apply to be a wedding consultant. This job is about getting out there and meeting people and convincing them that their day is the most important day in their life. They need to believe that if they want the day to be what they have dreamed it could be, then they need to hire you immediately.

This not to say that a wedding consultant should be pushy, because that turns people off. A wedding consultant must be inspiring. He or she must excite the imagination of a newly engaged bride-to-be and take her on the journey of her special day. Most brides-to-be are scared to death and having someone there to comfort and guide them is reassuring and worth paying for.

A successful wedding consultant must be patient, optimistic, and calm, no matter how stressful things may get. They must be, like Mary Poppins, prepared for any contingency and be able meet challenges with a sly smile that says it will be conquered.

Dos of Consulting

So what does a wedding consultant need to do to stay on top?

1. Be business minded

2. Be honest

3. Be creative

4. Be understanding

5. Be flexible

6. Be kind

7. Be strong

8. Be open minded

9. Be comforting

10. Be on time

Don'ts of Consulting

Here are some things that will sink a wedding consultant fast:

1. Be rude

2. Be impatient

3. Be unethical

4. Be bossy

5. Be a know-it-all

6. Be stiff

7. Be unavailable

8. Be uncaring

9. Be judgmental

10. Be unprepared

These are just some of the don'ts of being a wedding consultant. If you do not put an eye toward the business end of wedding consulting, you will not be able to keep afloat. It is a business and should be treated as such — with respect and commitment. Brides rely on you to create a beautiful day. In their eyes there is nothing you do not know about weddings or that you cannot do. So do not disappoint them. Stay on top of your game. Know what is going on in the industry and stay sharp when it comes to your competition.

What If I Do Not Like a Client Personally?

You do not have to like your clients. It is a business, not a place to make lifelong pals. There will be some friendships that will naturally occur, but if you have problems with a client, always keep in mind that after the happy day, you never have to deal with them again. You should think in terms of the bigger picture and try to get along the best way you can. You are working for money and this is a business transaction that you have agreed to for better or worse (you may have heard that phrase somewhere before).

If you determine at the beginning that you will have problems with the client, you need to make a decision of whether to work with them. If you can afford not to do that particular job, you can refer them elsewhere. You need to consider that if there continues to be a conflict or that it worsens, it could hurt your word-of-mouth business later.

Having a Bad Day

Everyone has a bad day now and then. What will get you through it is a sense of humor. You have to try to step back from a situation and look at it for what it is. Unfortunately, you cannot call in sick to a wedding. You have to grin and bear it, because the show must go on.

The professionals suggest that you always try to remain calm. This may be difficult, but being a wedding consultant can have its share of challenging days. There is a lot of stress, emotion, and drama that can surround a wedding. You should always try to diffuse it the best way you can. If you find that you are having more bad days than good days, you should consider taking a break and reevaluating your situation. Is this really what you want to be doing? Have you overbooked yourself? Have you scheduled enough breaks in between weddings? Have weddings dominated your life, and you are doing nothing else?

Keep in mind that you were hired to relieve the stress upon the bride, groom, and their families. If they see you having a bad day, you will make them have a bad day. If you need to go somewhere and scream into a pillow, do it. At the end of the day, two people will have the most wonderful day of their lives up to that point, and it is all because of you and your hard work. Pat yourself on the back occasionally. You deserve it.

Personality Traits That Can Harm Business

If you are the type of person that likes the spotlight on you, you are in the wrong business. Think of a wedding as a stage production. You have all of the actors — the bride, groom, family, close friends, bridesmaids, groomsmen, best man, maid of honor, flower girls. You have the stage — a church, a hotel, and a garden. You may have a couple of different acts — the parties, the wedding, the reception. The actors have their lines — vows, speeches. They even get to rehearse their production in which they learn their blocking — walking up the aisle, learning music cues, where to stand, where to sit. The sets are beautiful, lavish, and maybe even exotic. There is a dinner theater — so you get a meal and a show.

So where are you in this production that should be heading to Broadway? You are the director, stage manager, and backstage help. You are not the star; the bride is. If you want to be noticed and have a need to have yourself surrounded by adoring fans, then you may need to go to a real stage. For a wedding, you need to be in the background and make sure the production runs without a hitch. If there is a problem like a torn costume, then you need to fix it quickly so that no one notices.

The other personality trait that does not work well for a wedding consultant is if your feelings are easily hurt. In the heat of the moment, a bride may say some of the most awful things you have ever heard. You may just be the person she has chosen to unload on. You are an easy target, but more than that, a bride may trust that you are the one person that will not overreact to her meltdown. If you are easily offended by these outlandish displays of emotion, then wedding consulting is not for you. You can bet that you will be screamed at, blamed, and accused of trying to undermine a bride's day. When it is all over, more times than not you will get a hug, an apology, and a thanks.

If you have read this book from the beginning, you now should have all the necessary tools to become an awesome, brilliant, and highly successful wedding consultant. The next section contains case studies of wedding consultants — just like you — that talk frankly about their experiences and give you some sage advice about how to become as successful as they are.

Case Studies

Chapter 10

CASE STUDY: NIKKI KHAN

Exquisite Events

5635 Hazelcrest Circle

Westlake Village, CA 91362

Phone: 818-620-2665

Fax: 818-879-9115

Email: nikki@exquisevents.com

Web Page: www.exquisevents.com

Nikki always enjoyed throwing parties as far back as she can remember. After working as a volunteer for some organizations and working with an event production company, it seemed natural for her to start her own wedding consulting business.

What did it cost Nikki to begin her new venture? She invested $10,000 to begin her business on the right foot. Her business originally grew by word of mouth. This year she is beginning to advertise Exquisite Events in local magazines and some sites on the Internet. She states that most of her business still comes from referrals from previous clients.

Here is Nikki's advice for upcoming brides. When planning a wedding, a bride should consider the size of the wedding and the number of events involved. Based on this information, wedding plans should begin anywhere from six months to one year beforehand. If the wedding family wants to come and enjoy their son or daughter's wedding as a guest, it is crucial to have a consultant. Your whole day will be micromanaged from managing the vendors, photographers, and videographer to taking the key photo at special moments to planning the ceremony and reception schedule so the event flows smoothly and successfully.

She has even more detailed suggestions for new wedding consultants. When it comes to working with difficult brides or families, she suggests that you always act professional and not let your emotions get in the way. Try not to take personally things that they may say to you in the heat of the moment. If your heart is into it, and you can handle the stress of the bride, her family, and the groom and his family, and you can play the role of a confidante, adviser, and remain professional throughout the process, then you are ready to be a successful wedding consultant. Nikki suggests that a wedding consultant go to as many meetings, industry events, and networking events as possible and always stay on top of trends.

When clients have unrealistic expectations such as calling you anytime day or night and expecting an immediate response, this can be stressful for a wedding consultant. Nikki reveals that she has had clients that have called her at 11 p.m. or 7 a.m. and were totally stressed out. She handled them like a pro with kid gloves and made them feel like she was on their side and that she would do anything to make their wedding day special.

When surprises happen during the process of planning a wedding, Nikki states that you have to remain calm and do the best that you can. Nikki shares a story of the time when the linen company failed to show up on time. She kept her cool and asked the disc jockey if he had any fabric for the backdrop in his car. He rescued her by quickly creating a backdrop which the client did not even notice. She managed to pull it off a few minutes before opening the ballroom doors. She only survived by keeping calm and quickly coming up with a solution.

In the area of finances, Nikki has her husband work out her taxes and file them once a year. She says that her business plan includes a budget, goals, and a business forecast. Exquisite Events offers three different packages. The first one is called A-Z and is their all-inclusive package. In this package the client chooses the décor elements and then Nikki will do a mock table setup in the actual venue with the chosen linens, chairs, flowers, and lighting.

Their second package is called Fill In the Blanks. In this package the client already has a few vendors picked out but needs help with securing some others as well as tying up loose ends.

CASE STUDY: NIKKI KHAN

The third package is called "The Day Of...." With this package Nikki will gather all of the information concerning the vendors that the client has hired and will communicate with them the week of the wedding. Nikki will be the first one at the venue and the last one to leave on the day of the event. Exquisite Events will make sure the schedule runs smoothly and will manage all of the vendors in order to orchestrate the event.

Nikki runs her wedding consulting business from her home. Her office is detached from her house, and has a computer, Internet access, a fax machine, and a separate phone line. Nikki states that having good organizational skills and a good, trusting personality are essential to her success.

What is in Nikki's emergency kit?

It contains bobby pins, hair pins, Kleenex, Tylenol, Epsom salts, nail polish remover, hard candy, a fresh packet of crackers, and hair spray to name a few items. Nail polish remover has often come in handy for little tears in the pantyhose and safety pins are invaluable for some last-minute adjustments for the bridal party. If the bride is feeling queasy, it helps to have hard candy and crackers.

CASE STUDY: CHYRILL SANDRINI

Chyrill Sandrini

SANDRINI CONCEPTS WEDDINGS & EVENTS

Owner – Coordinator

1918 G Street

Bakersfield, CA 93301

Phone 661-322-7074

www.sandriniconcepts.com

Chyrill@sandriniconcepts.com

Chyrill is a mother of three that had never thought she would end up becoming a wedding consultant. She had worked in law enforcement for 17 years at four different agencies. An injury on the job changed her life. As part of an assessment to find a new line of work, Chyrill discovered she had an aptitude for event planning. A job opportunity as a wedding consultant became available and she began her exciting journey.

She began with a budget of $5,000 to start up her business. This was to pay for a Web site, business cards, a desk, a computer and printer, and a business phone line. Her budget soon was overrun when the first item on her list, creating a Web site which included a blog, cost her over $2,100. This did not daunt her spirit and Sandrini Concepts is now doing 50 events a year.

Chyrill started small as a home-based business. After three years she moved to an 1,100-square-foot office and now is looking to move again because she has outgrown the space.

Chyrill has learned a lot along the way and is constantly learning what it takes to be a successful wedding planner. She does have some tips and words of wisdom for aspiring wedding consultants.

When starting out, Chyrill recommends that you spend the necessary time to research your market. This includes finding out how many competitors you have. Next she recommends that you decide how committed you will be — will it be full time or part time? She has learned that it takes hard work and dedication to gain the confidence of her clients and the community she lives in. Make sure that you have the necessary equipment to make wedding consulting a breeze. Here is a list of what she recommends:

CASE STUDY: CHYRILL SANDRINI

- Cell phone

- Radio communication for onsite use

- Emergency kit for the event

- Computer

- Fax

- Printer

- Desk

- Filing cabinet

- Plastic containers

- An area large enough to store all of your supplies and equipment

Chyrill has had her share of difficult clients. Her recommendation is that you should always try to remain calm, polite, and respectful. If a wedding consultant makes the bride feel that she is important and that her day is a priority, this will often diffuse most situations. She recommends that you do not let brides see how stressed you are, because they may see this as a cue to panic since they are relying on you. Be assertive when you need to, listen to the client, and be ready to make a plan.

Planning ahead is what Chyrill recommends the most. She states that you can count on an emergency happening. She has the phone numbers of rental companies and other vendors ready on her cell phone in case the worst happens. Because she was prepared, a wedding was saved when an unexpected rain threatened to ruin a wedding that was set up outside for 432 guests. She got busy and used the resources she had at her fingertips. After a call, 20 men and a dry tent were put into place and the bride and groom had a wedding reception to remember.

When asked why a bride should use a wedding coordinator, Chyrill replies that hiring a wedding coordinator gives peace of mind. A wedding coordinator is a "go-to" person, a shoulder to lean on, and has the experience to plan, coordinate, design, and execute a wedding.

Chyrill does not use a business plan. Rather, she prefers rather to learn from experience. She has a lot of "I won't do that again" experiences. She is trying to evolve a plan, but just is not there yet.

CASE STUDY: CHYRILL SANDRINI

Chyrill does business a little differently from her competitors. Sandrini Concepts' minimum for full event coordination is $3,000. They do not offer packages, but instead listen to their clients' needs and they then price the event according to staffing, work time, and products they may need to supply. Chyrill's philosophy is that it is rude to make a client fit into a package they may not need.

Here are some thoughts from Chyrill to help you create a smashing wedding consultant business:

- Always be on top of your game. Stay current with the trends and create new ideas and experiences for your client.

- Expect long hours and physical work. It is not easy setting up and taking down tables and chairs week after week. Realize that your staff will only work as hard as you set the example for them to follow.

- Start small, take a lot of photos, and never burn a bridge you might need to cross again. Introduce yourself to vendors and let them know you are in the business.

- Invest in a bridal show; they bring you a captive audience who is looking for your services.

- Consider using a great name — something that is branded and sets you apart. Take your cards into vendor shops such as photographers, cake decorators, and rental companies.

Sandrini Concepts is the wedding consultant for the Majestic Fox Theater (**www.foxtheateronline.com**), an expert event coordinator for the *Bakersfield Californian* newspaper, and has award-winning table designs. They have won first place for wedding Web site of the year.

What's in Chyrill's emergency kit? Here are some of her comments:

"The emergency kit seems to grow at each event. Here are some of the basics: First, we use a rolling cart; I believe they originally started at Office Depot stores for those who had to wheel big files, especially lawyers. Then a couple of years ago, Sam's Club or Costco started offering a rolling cart that had an insert with tons of pockets and dividers — I believe for scrapbooking materials. We saw it as our emergency cart on wheels. We also use fishing tackle boxes for all of the small things like safety pins of all sizes, needles, thread, Krazy Glue, and more essential sewing stuff."

CASE STUDY: CHYRILL SANDRINI

"We actually have two kits so we can manage two events on one day, but we also bring them both so one is always at the reception site and then one goes to the wedding venue.

"Some other items in our emergency kit are: extension cords, fire clickers, Tums, Benadryl, Tylenol, more stomach aids, bandages, scissors, female items, breath mints, groom's socks in black and brown, garters, ring pillow (you may laugh but it has come in handy — a small ring pillow in white will always do the trick), tape, double-sided tape, a couple pairs of nylons, wire, rope, stain remover sticks, wipes, batteries, pens and paper, and a map of the area we are in if we are out of town. And of course since I am prior law enforcement, I also have breathing masks in case I need to perform CPR. At every event it seems we add something, but it has been a lifesaver!

"You know you are the hero when you can sew a bridesmaid in a dress — on your knees in the limo — before the wedding. My assistant Cathi had to hold the dress I sewed (remember, you need to carry every color of thread you can think of to do this). Cathi got a leg cramp in the limo, and I yelled not to let go of the dress as she stuck her leg out into the face of the bride. It was hilarious and we laugh at this all the time. The wedding started six minutes later, and the bridesmaid dress stayed all the way through the reception — dancing, everything! Now it was not the prettiest sew job upon examination, but it worked, and I am sure someone had to cut her out of the dress!"

This photo was taken at a Table Top Shootout competition at Girari Fine Furnishings in Beverly Hills. Sandrini Concepts had an award-winning table and they were selected to compete against the big hitters! They were the only coordination firm that was not planning movie star weddings, the Oscar parties, or another gala.

CASE STUDY: DAWN PAPPAS

Lili's Concept

12109 Ridgefield Parkway

Richmond, VA 23238

Phone: 804-741-5454

Hours are by appointment only.

Offers everything from consulting to full coordination.

Also a salon and spa, offering bridal packages for makeup, hair, and other spa services.

Dawn M. Pappas graduated from Redford Union High School in 1998. Her first exposure to planning and executing events came much earlier in her life. Her aunt, who is a caterer, had her assist in the preparation and servicing of various events. This gave her a hands-on experience in managing group events. This experience allowed her to meet more people and service more functions. Because of this exposure, more family, friends, and friends of friends began requesting her services.

These working experiences prompted her to launch her own wedding and event planning business in 2002, Fairy Tale Events, which she owned and operated for four years. While running this business she worked as a mentor and a career advisor for U.S. Event Guide, an online certification school. She then moved on to become an Executive Assistant and Consultant for Lili's Concept in Richmond, Virginia, and she continues to mentor for the online certification school. She continues to balance work at the office and online while taking care of her family: her husband Nick, daughter Aryanna, and her one-year-old son, Lukas.

When asked why she decided to take the plunge and become a wedding planner, Dawn replied that it happened through a process that started when she was very young. She explains that she always had a knack for planning and executing various events. It started out as a hobby helping her friends and family plan birthday parties, Christmas parties, and weddings. This interest soon grew into a passion which sparked her desire to develop event planning as a career.

When Dawn decided to open up her own business, she chose to specialize in weddings because she wanted to help couples be able to create the wedding of their dreams and still enjoy their engagement. Dawn wanted to be able to help them create a wedding to remember that expressed who they were as a couple, but without all of the stress and headache this can entail.

CASE STUDY: DAWN PAPPAS

Dawn disclosed that she invested around $5,000 to begin her event planning business. She recommends that it is necessary for all wedding consultants to have a cell phone, business cards, a computer, contact management software, an appointment book and calendar, a wedding emergency kit, wedding software for professional wedding planners, a smile, and a friendly personality.

Dawn offers packages that range from consulting to the complete package, which can include purchasing the wedding gown to the flower arrangements at the event. She also offers a customized package option so couples can include only services that they need. All of her packages are priced at a flat rate with the smallest package including three hours of service and the biggest package including over 100 hours. At the end of the year, like a lot of wedding consultants, Dawn leaves it to the tax professionals to do her taxes.

Dawn offers some advice to wedding consultants breaking into the business. She states that one of the most important things is to get as much experience as possible. She states that a person can read all of the wedding books in the world and watch many wedding-related television shows, but nothing prepares you better to enter this field than on-the-job training. She suggests that a person who is really interested in gaining expereince can begin by just volunteering to help coordinate or plan different events and activities through their family, church, or community.

Dawn also suggests that a wedding consultant seek out a professional school that offers wedding or event planning training. Dawn was certified in Wedding Planning in October 2002, and certified in Events in July of 2003. She is currently pursuing a certificate in Special Events and Interior Design which she will complete in the fall of 2008.

Once wedding consultants have gained some experience and have been formally trained, Dawn suggests that they need to network with other professionals in the wedding business, and other types of businesses, in order to get their names out there. She suggests that it is also very beneficial to join wedding associations. Using creative marketing techniques that leave a lasting impression will also help consultants to get their names out there as well.

In addition, Dawn suggests that sending out press releases about your company or holding a grand opening for your new business is a good way to advertise. She states that holding wedding workshops are also great venues that can help a wedding consultant gain exposure.

CASE STUDY: DAWN PAPPAS

Dawn advertises mainly online because so many brides are looking for the services that they need for their wedding online, where they can get an idea of what is offered before they even meet a coordinator.

Dawn also has some advice concerning brides and their families. Dawn states that she handles difficult brides or families by remaining professional and trying to be empathetic with what they are going through. She goes on to say that if you can try to put yourself in their shoes, you can relate to how they are feeling and then you can come up with some solutions to remedy the situation.

Dawn feels a family should use a wedding planner because this should be an enjoyable time for all involved. The couple should enjoy their engagement and not have to worry about all of the stress involved with planning a wedding. Dawn suggests that brides should plan their wedding at least ten months in advance.

When a family hires a wedding planner, it is very helpful to have an advisor to assist in creating a wedding of their dreams, and someone to listen to all of their ideas and give them professional advice. A wedding consultant can save the couple time because the wedding planner has experience planning weddings and has developed a relationship with many vendors. This also leads to a cost savings as Dawn can often purchase the items they need at a lower cost.

Dawn feels all families can benefit from a wedding planner on the day of, because if you have a professional to oversee all of the details and orchestrate and execute that day, everyone can be a guest at their own event. A bride cannot truly enjoy her event if she is worrying if everything is running on time, everyone is where they need to be, and everything is being set up correctly. A professional wedding planner can handle all of those details and then the family and the bride can enjoy the day they have been looking forward to.

Wedding consulting is hard work. Dawn says the most difficult thing about being a wedding planner is trying to deal with clients or families who are hard to please. She further states that in this wedding business, you have to work with so many people and they all have different personalities. You just have to remain professional at all times and always keep your client's best interest at heart.

Sometimes things do not always go as planned. When the unexpected happens, Dawn will have a Plan B ready. If she is having an outdoor wedding, she always makes sure there is an indoor facility available to use in case of rain or other unforeseen acts of God. Dawn tries to prepare for the unexpected and an emergency kit has come in handy many times.

CASE STUDY: DAWN PAPPAS

Sometimes the unexpected can be funny. Dawn recounts one of these experiences — a flower girl who refused to walk down the aisle without a leading trail of M&M's. She was only three years old and the only way they could coax her to walk down the aisle was to put her favorite candy out.

What is in Dawn's emergency kit? She responds:

"My emergency kit is divided into three different sections: for me, bride and bridesmaids, and groom and groomsmen. I have two over-the-door organizers and in each pocket I have items my clients may need to use. I hang them on the door of the room the bride is getting ready in and the door of the room the groom is getting ready in. When everyone is ready I put everything back in my rolling suitcase and I can pull it out and hang it up if anyone needs anything later that day."

My Bag

- Two veils — one in ivory and one in white (both elbow length)
- Cake server set
- Blank guestbook
- Flower girl basket
- Ring bearer pillow
- Toasting flutes
- Schedule and directions to the event
- Three different-style tiaras
- Hair dryer
- Small iron
- Curling iron
- Scissors
- Krazy Glue
- Sewing kit
- Chalk
- Shout wipes

CASE STUDY: DAWN PAPPAS

- Safety pins
- Static cling spray
- Masking tape
- Scotch Tape
- Duct tape
- Markers
- Colored pencils
- Notepad
- Measuring tape
- Ribbon
- Tulle
- Corsage pins
- Smelling salts
- Instant ice pack
- Bandages
- Sunscreen
- Insect repellent
- Flashlight
- Wet wipes
- Garbage bags
- Trail mix
- Umbrella

Brides' and Bridesmaids' Kit

- Beauty aids
- Baby powder
- Blush

CASE STUDY: DAWN PAPPAS

- Bobby pins
- Breath mints
- Combs
- Lip balm
- Clear nail polish
- Deodorant
- Earring backings
- Eyelash curler
- Floss
- Hair spray
- Hair ties
- Mouthwash
- Toothbrush
- Toothpaste
- Makeup kit
- Makeup remover
- Nail clippers
- Nail file
- New hairbrushes
- Tweezers
- Hand lotion
- Cotton swabs
- Kleenex

Health

- Anti-diarrhea medication
- Bandages

CASE STUDY: DAWN PAPPAS

- Cough drops

- Cough medicine, nondrowsy formula

- Throat spray

- Tums

- Tylenol

- Neosporin

- Trail mix

- Saltine crackers

- Hard candy

- Mini-cheese/cracker snacks

Grooms' and Groomsmen's Kit

- Black dress socks

- Shoe polish

- Extra black shoelaces

- Kleenex

- Hairspray

- Gel

- Nail file

- Nail clippers

- New hair brush

- Men's deodorant

- Lip balm

- Hand lotion

- Cotton swabs

- Mouthwash

CASE STUDY: DAWN PAPPAS

- Breath mints
- Toothbrush
- Toothpaste
- Floss

Health

- Anti-diarrhea medication
- Bandages
- Cough drops
- Cough medicine, nondrowsy formula
- Throat spray
- Tums
- Tylenol
- Neosporin
- Trail mix
- Saltine crackers
- Hard candy
- Mini-cheese/cracker snacks

"My kit has come in handy at several weddings. I once had to have my assistant use my sewing kit to hem two bridesmaids' dresses, as they failed to have their dresses hemmed, and they thought if they wore higher heels it would be fine. They were wrong and when they showed up to get ready, they were tripping on their dresses. Lucky for me my assistant used to be a seamstress."

CASE STUDY: JESSICA H. GREENSTEIN

Certified Wedding Planner

**President of A Perfect Day Wedding
& Event Coordinators**

**202-459-4704 Baltimore/Washington D.C.
metro office phone**

772-224-8145 South Florida phone

561-512-7013 Cell phone

561-828-0286 Fax

Info@aperday.com E-mail

www.aperday.com

Jessica never wanted to become a wedding planner; consequently, she accidentally fell into the business. A few years ago, Jessica was focused on becoming an attorney; however, she had family in the wedding industry. One of her best friends in college had always wanted to be a wedding planner, and one day she came to Jessica with an engagement ring on her finger and Jessica said, "I guess we need to start planning." Jessica had so much fun "planning" the wedding that she thought she should do it for "real" and plan weddings for profit. Jessica promised to handle the business end of things, and agreed to back the business financially, if her friend would do the creative side. It's several years later, and Jessica's friend's wedding never took place, but Jessica still has a thriving wedding planning business to show for it, and now Jessica is active in all facets of the business.

Jessica's investment was a little over $5,000, almost half of which went into her Web site. The additional expenses included licensing, insurance, and advertising. She states that working from home and doing consultations in clients' homes or a coffee shop kept the overhead low. If she has an appointment for a menu tasting or a floral consultation, she takes the bride to the vendor. Otherwise, all of her business is completed by phone, fax, and e-mail.

On the business end of things, Jessica has a business plan that includes profit projections, cost of doing business, cash flow analysis, marketing strategies, and essentially her firm's résumé. Jessica files her personal taxes individually and her business taxes are filed with the personal taxes as a sole proprietorship. All employees with her firm are independent contractors and for them she files a Form 1099.

CASE STUDY: JESSICA H. GREENSTEIN

Jessica offers some advice for wedding consultants both new and veteran:

"My best advice for someone trying to break into the business is to have patience. This is two-fold; to be successful, it takes time. You may have to beat the pavement to market yourself until you feel like you are ready to drop, but with time and patience, the efforts are very rewarding. Second, you must have patience with your clients. Getting married is a very emotional time for your clients and their families. Some brides are withdrawn from the shock of the idea that they are getting married; others are high-strung, intense, and obsessed with every last detail. The latter ones will make you want to shave your head, but keep in mind the experiences that you will gain from the opportunity to plan their wedding. I am not saying that you will never get great clients. At least a few times a year, I have clients that I adore and with whom I have become really close friends; however, you will never be completely free of the variety of hair-pulling personalities, not just in the brides, but their mothers, and even their aunts. This is why the greatest advice I can give is to have patience.

"To get your name out there, you have to first and foremost market yourself. Next, you need to give your services away. I know that is discouraging to hear, but in the beginning you cannot expect to make a lot of money until you establish your reputation. Understandably, you have to prove yourself in your field. Finally, you need to build up clientele, testimonials, and pictures from your weddings for your portfolio.

"In order to be a successful wedding consultant, you must arm yourself with the following things: a computer with high-speed Internet access, a fax machine, cell phone, a Web site, business cards, a portfolio, an emergency kit, a great contract, a creative mind, good business sense, the ability to laugh at yourself and take defeat easily, and out-of-this-world people skills."

When faced with a difficult client, Jessica offers the following wisdom:

"I have found that my best defense for a difficult bride and/or their families is a good offense. Knowing your client's likes, dislikes, and personalities is the first step to preventing a negative situation. For example: The other day I met one of my favorite clients (we'll call her Abby), her mother (we'll call her Jan), her future mother-in-law (we'll call her Mary), and her future father-in-law (we'll call him George) at a linen rental company to select linens for her wedding. The rental company had previously set up some tables with Abby's colors. Abby and Jan were running late, but Mary and George were on time. Mary came inside and took a look at the tables and instantly fell in love with one of them. It was a burnt orange cotton tablecloth with these frilly little bobs hanging from every square

CASE STUDY: JESSICA H. GREENSTEIN

inch of it. She asked me for my opinion, to which I told her that although I thought it was pretty, I thought it would be a little too frou-frou for the bride because she likes things more simple, and the fluffy little decorations would probably not fly. For five minutes she continued to try to get me to agree with her about how beautiful and unique the tablecloth was and how much the bride would love it. Trust me, Mary was relentless. Finally Abby showed up and when Mary asked her what she thought of the tablecloth Abby stared at it for a few minutes, and then told Mary almost verbatim what I had said to her about it. After that, Mary said to me, 'Wow, you were right. You really do know her well.' This example is just one of the many simple ways you can 'know' your client. Other ways include not suggesting hot pink when the colors are aqua and silver or not suggesting something environmentally extravagant to a client that wants to 'go green.' I find that it also helps to try to look at things from the outside in; do not be afraid to step out of your comfort zone. I always tell my clients that I will give them the pros and cons, I'll play devil's advocate with them, and I'll give them my professional opinion, but in the end the decision is theirs. I have found that because I do not get my personal opinion involved, I don't butt heads with my clients. If all else fails, step back and count to ten. Remember, you're being paid, you've got a job to do, and next time — charge more!"

Jessica states that word of mouth is the best advertisement and endorsement for wedding consulting businesses. Additionally, she states that she has a Web site to drive traffic as well as various other wedding-related Web sites and lead-generating sites. She is networked with other vendors and is a preferred vendor at many hotels. Jessica says that her firm also participates in a wide variety of press opportunities in order to gain publicity.

Different companies offer different wedding planning packages. At A Perfect Day Wedding & Event Coordinators they offer a variety of different services and prices associated with those packages. A "Day Of" package can be as low as $600 and includes a site walk-through, schedule, confirmation of vendors, and setup and orchestration the day of the wedding. Rehearsals and chair cover setup are additional and certain details such as wedding date, number of guests, and size of their bridal party affect the price of the package as well. The next package up is the "Partial Planning" package, which starts at $2,000 and is a scaled-down version of the "Complete Planning" package. The "Complete Planning" package starts at $3,000 and goes up from there depending on various factors including those above as well as the elaborateness of the wedding, number of vendors, and location of the wedding, if travel is needed. It is not unusual for a large, elaborate wedding to be charged a $12,000 commission. The "Complete Planning" package includes everything from selecting invitations to assistance

CASE STUDY: JESSICA H. GREENSTEIN

with honeymoon planning, selecting their photographer to choosing favors, and everything in between. This is a fully comprehensive package.

Sometimes there are unexpected situations that may arise that a wedding consultant must be prepared for. Jessica states that dealing with unexpected situations can be stressful, but with patience, proper training, and discipline, any situation can be overcome. She is happy to say that with part of her business in a market that sees so much rain, she has never had to move an outside ceremony or reception indoors due to weather. This is extremely rare given the amount of rain that falls in South Florida. However, for those unfortunate occasions such as the cake icing being displaced during travel, vendors failing to show, or a smudge on the bridesmaid's dress, she comes prepared. For the cake, if it is buttercream, it can easily be molded back together. If the cake is fondant, a pastry brush and some melted butter — or worst-case scenario, a damp paper towel — will do the trick. For a no-show vendor, Jessica has a backup list of vendors in each category ready to go. Lastly, for a smudge, she carries a complete emergency kit with "Shout wipes" and fabric cleaner pens.

Jessica believes strongly that a bride should plan ahead and use a wedding consultant. Ideally, a bride should start planning her wedding a year in advance. If she has more time, wonderful, but the anticipation may start to get to her after a while. Six to nine months is still doable, but they may not have first choice when it comes to venue and vendor selection. Jessica states that anything less than six months, although possible and she has certainly done it before, is absolute mayhem and can become extremely stressful and rushed.

Jessica believes that wedding planners are more of a necessity than a luxury nowadays. She believes this because of all the benefits that a wedding consultant brings, and most other vendors will agree that involving a wedding planner makes things easier. First of all, the time saved by using a planner is absolutely rewarding. The average wedding takes 40 hours to plan, and that is not including the time it takes to research vendors, the format of a wedding, and religious traditions. Wedding planners already know the reputable vendors and their prices, what goes into planning a wedding, what needs to be done, and the traditions families may want to follow if they are of a certain religion. Second, the creativity that wedding planners have is insurmountable. Most are trained to know what colors go with what and how to go about meeting a client's tastes and needs. Additionally, think about the peace of mind you will be providing your clients knowing that they have a professional looking out for their best interests and ensuring that everything gets done in time. Finally, the money that can be saved through exclusive offers or negotiation can often more than cover the cost of hiring a wedding planner itself.

CASE STUDY: JESSICA H. GREENSTEIN

Jessica prides herself on being able to make the whole stressful process of planning a wedding as lighthearted and fun as possible. She cracks jokes, laughs, and tries to keep things as smooth sailing as she can. As an example, Jessica recalls a funny moment:

"A few years ago, I had a wedding that took place at the bride and groom's home — a gorgeous, multimillion-dollar, Spanish-style villa on the Intercoastal in North Miami Beach. As we ended the evening, the couple's dogs were helping the caterers by prerinsing the dishes, which was followed by ten or so drunken wedding guests who decided to go for a midnight swim in the newlyweds' pool in the backyard. I just remember staring in awe, trying not to laugh as the one dog circled the pool repeatedly before doing cannonballs into the pool and soaking the linens that were still on the tables."

Here are some final thoughts from Jessica:

"The most difficult thing about being a wedding coordinator, besides the long hours and ridiculous deadlines, is the inability to make everyone happy. Forget it right now; it will *never* happen! Your main goal is to make the bride and/or whoever hired you happy; anyone else is just a bonus! There will always be parents, in-laws, grandparents, extended families, and friends who complain about something. Whether it's the food, the ceremony start time, the room temperature, the assigned seats, or the volume of the music, you will never be able to reach absolute perfection. Strive for it, but do not feel defeated when it is not achieved."

After starting A Perfect Day a few years ago in the D.C. area, Jessica decided to open a satellite office in South Florida, which quickly bloomed into a fully functional office. Jessica now spends her time traveling between both.

What is in Jessica's emergency kit?

- Aspirin

- Breath mints, gum, or Tic Tacs

- Bottled water

- Snacks (crackers, cheese, grapes)

- Extra makeup (cover-up, lipstick)

- Hand mirror

- Hair spray

Case Study: Jessica H. Greenstein

- Hand lotion
- Cotton swabs
- Tissues
- Tampons
- Clear nail polish
- Nail file
- Extra pairs of nylons
- Safety pins
- Masking tape
- Stapler
- Small sewing kit
- First-aid kit
- Smelling salts
- Pen and small notepad
- Contact numbers for vendors
- Bandages
- Deodorant
- Barrettes and bobby pins
- Perfume
- Visine
- Krazy Glue
- Toothpicks
- Nondrowsy allergy medicines
- Shout wipes
- Prescription meds for the bride and groom
- Chalk

CASE STUDY: JESSICA H. GREENSTEIN

- Drinking straws

- Comb and brush

- Hair gel and wax

- Clorox bleach pen

- Antacids

CASE STUDY: DAWN COWART

Dawn Cowart

Traditionally Modern Wedding Planners

Member, Association of Bridal Consultants

2510 Ashbourne Drive

Lawrenceville, GA 30043

678-300-2124

www.traditionallymodern.com

My name is Dawn Cowart and I am a professional wedding coordinator. I have been planning weddings for the past twenty years, but professionally — for money — for the past five years. Working together with my assistant (and sister) Debbie O'Neal, we plan events that our clients can be a "guest" at. I take all the worry and stress out of wedding planning.

I am a mother of three teenagers — and yes, I still have all of my own hair — and have been married to the same man for the past twenty years. I have coached recreational cheerleading for the past ten years and I enjoy every moment of it. I take life one day at a time and remember that God is in complete control so I am just trucking along for the ride. I love my family and I love my job; what else could I ask for?

I wanted to become a planner because I love working in an environment where my creativity is used. I began my business with very little money. I already had a computer and home office so I didn't need very much. In order to advertise I used all of the "free" vendor listings on wedding sites. I am on Getmarried.com and some local advertising as well. Word of mouth is the best advertising. Talk about your business wherever you are.

CASE STUDY: DAWN COWART

The advice I would give to someone trying to break into the business is to be patient and work hard. Take it slow and pray! There will be times that things do not go as planned. Deal with it. Things will happen and if you cannot handle the pressure, you need to rethink this business. Things can be difficult at times, such as trying to convince a bride that what she wants is 'tacky'!

I try to deal with everything with humor that will take the edge off. Sometimes unexpected things can be amusing, like the time I watched a flower girl sit down in the middle of the aisle runner.

I always try to handle difficult brides or families with patience. I always try to remember that this is my job, but it is one of the most important days of the bride and groom's life. I try to keep them calm and work through whatever problems come up.

My services begin at $3,000 and go up from there. For that price, a family will receive everything they need. I have several packages. When asked whether I offer anything special with my packages I reply, "I am something special!"

I believe that brides should begin planning from about one year in advance. I do not book anything less than full coordination more than one year in advance.

I believe my services save a bride money, stress, time, and sanity.

I do have a business plan that includes my goals and how I intend to achieve them. For my taxes I use an accountant.

I believe that wedding consultants need to "talk, talk, talk" to be known in the community. In addition, they should join a leads club and the Association of Bridal Consultants.

For a wedding consultant to begin, he or she should have a separate phone line, a private place to conduct business, a laptop computer, business cards that give pertinent information, and a *great* assistant.

State Bridal Shows

Appendix A

Here is a list of different annual bridal shows broken down by the states in which they occur.

Alabama

http://www.alabamabridal.com/events.asp

This site has listing of bridal shows all around Alabama.

Alaska

http://www.alaskabride.com/weddingfair2008.html

This is an annual show in Anchorage.

Arizona

http://www.bridalfashiondebut.com/shows.html

This is a large show in the Phoenix area.

Arkansas

http://www.arkansasonline.com/bridalfair/more_conway.html

This show is sponsored by a newspaper in Arkansas. There are two events.

California

http://www.bridalshowcase-ca.com

This is a link to a number of shows around the state.

Colorado

http://www.rockymtnbridalshow.com

This is in the Denver area.

Connecticut

http://www.myconnecticutwedding.com/common/events

This site lists Connecticut bridal shows as well as those in surrounding states.

Delaware

http://www.wedalert.com/bridal_show/bridalshow.asp?state=DE

This site lists a number of shows in the state as well as some other states as well.

Florida

http://floridaweddingexpo.com

This site offers a number of shows around Florida.

Georgia

http://www.atleventshow.com

This site has a number of links to bridal shows in the Atlanta area.

Hawaii

http://www.bridesclub.com/bridal-shows/hawaii-bridal-expo-january.cfm

This site has a show in Honolulu. This company does shows all around the United States.

Idaho

http://www.abridalextravaganza.com

This is a large show in Boise.

Illinois

http://www.bridalexpochicago.com

This site has a number of bridal expos in the Chicago and Milwaukee areas.

Indiana

http://www.lovingtouchbridalboutique.com

This site has listings of upcoming bridal events in Indiana.

http://www.indianabridalguide.com/TopLevel/BridalShows.htm

This site has a comprehensive list of bridal shows and links for wedding consultants.

Iowa

http://www.yourweddingiowa.com/forum.html

This is a show in the Des Moines area.

Kansas

http://www.wichitabridalshow.com/shows.html

This site has information on a bridal show in Wichita.

Kentucky

http://www.lexingtonbridalshows.com

This has a couple of shows in the Lexington area.

Louisiana

http://www.weddingswithstyle.net/shows3.php#LA

This is a magazine-sponsored site. It has a number of shows in Louisiana and other states as well.

Maine

http://pbmaine.com/shows.php

This site has information about bridal shows in Maine and New Hampshire.

Maryland

http://www.pureinheartweddings.com

This is a show in Hanover, Maryland.

Massachusetts

> **http://www.pureinheartweddings.com**

This site has a few shows in Massachusetts.

Michigan

> **http://www.bridestobeshows.net/shows.asp**

This site has listings of shows all over Michigan.

> **http://www.whimsicaloccasions.com/EventsPage.htm**

This site also has bridal shows throughout Michigan.

Minnesota

> **http://www.twincitybridal.com/wedding_fair.html**

This site features a show in the St. Paul area.

Mississippi

> **http://www.msbridalshowandexpo.com**

This site has a show in Jackson.

Missouri

> **http://www.bridesclub.com/wedding/st-louis-weddings/bridal-show.cfm**

This site has a show in St. Louis.

Montana

http://www.kzoq.com/modules.php?name=Content&pa=showpage&pid=43

This is a radio station–sponsored wedding fair in western Montana.

Nebraska

http://omahabridalnetwork.com

This site has information about a show in Omaha and other surrounding states as well.

Nevada

http://renobridalshow.com

This site promotes a bridal show in Reno.

New Hampshire

http://www.countrybridals.com/bridalevents.html

This site has local events listed in New Hampshire.

New Jersey

http://www.americanbride.com/bridalshowsnj.htm?gclid=CPn90_LN_pACFQ9hgQodtjT11g

This site has a list of a number of different bridal shows in New Jersey.

New Mexico

http://www.premierbridenewmexico.com/bridal-shows.htm

This site has a number of bridal shows in New Mexico.

New York

http://www.bridaltradeshows.com

This site has New York bridal shows as well as bridal shows in nearby states.

North Carolina

http://www.foreverbridal.net

This site has listings of bridal shows in the Raleigh area.

http://www.freewebs.com/lauramassie/bridalshowcase.htm

This site has shows listed in the Charlotte area.

North Dakota

http://www.kfyrtv.com/Bridal%20Show.htm

This is a television station–sponsored show in Bismarck.

Ohio

http://www.claiborneproductions.com

This site has a number of shows around Ohio.

Oklahoma

http://www.okbride.com

This site lists bridal shows in central Oklahoma.

Oregon

http://oregonweddingshowcase.com

This site promotes shows near Eugene.

Pennsylvania

http://www.osbornejenks.com/pabridal.html

This site has a show in Lehigh Valley.

Rhode Island

http://www.bostonbridalshows.com/rhodeislandbridalshows. html

This site promotes a bridal show in Newport.

South Carolina

http://www.southcarolinabride.com/Bridalshows.htm

This site has a number of different shows listed for South Carolina.

South Dakota

http://www.siouxfallsevents.com/eventDetails. CFM?EventID=7695

This is a fundraising bridal show in Sioux Falls.

Tennessee

http://www.midsouthweddingshow.com

This site has bridal show listings in the Germantown area of Tennessee.

Texas

http://www.4starevents.com

This site has listings in the Dallas area of bridal shows.

Utah

http://www.utahbrides.com/bridalshows.php

This site promotes a bridal show in Salt Lake City.

Vermont

http://burlingtonvtbridalshow.com

This site promotes a few different seasonal bridal shows in Vermont.

Virginia

http://www.showbride.com

This site has listings of bridal shows all around Virginia.

http://www.eventsavvi.com

This site has a listing of three or four bridal show events in Virginia.

Washington

http://www.bridesclub.com/wedding/seattle-weddings/bridal-show.cfm

This site has a couple of bridal shows in Seattle.

West Virginia

http://www.charlestonwvciviccenter.com/wedding.htm

This site promotes a show in Charleston.

Wisconsin

http://wisconsinbridalshows.com

This site has a number of bridal shows in Wisconsin.

Wyoming

http://www.celebrationbridalshows.com/index.htm

This site has shows in various places in Wyoming.

The listings about bridal shows change often. A good place to find updated information is **http://www.wedalert.com/bridal_show**.

Business Plan Sample

Appendix B

XYZ Wedding Consultants'

Business Plan

Executive Summary

XYZ Wedding Consultants is a company that provides comprehensive wedding planning and services related to weddings. XYZ has one wedding consultant, Sarah, who is experienced in providing wedding services and has training and certification in the areas of catering and wedding planning. XYZ gives each client their full attention and Sarah actively listens, then designs each wedding individually rather than working from a cookie-cutter script. Sarah treats each bride the way she would want to be treated for her wedding or those of her own daughters. If XYZ cannot create the specified wedding in the time needed, XYZ will turn the job down and recommend another qualified consultant. XYZ wants each bride to get exactly what she wants and deserves and if that means the bride finds it somewhere else, then XYZ is dedicated to providing her with that option. Included in XYZ's wedding services are weddings, honeymoons, receptions, budget planning, and answers to etiquette questions. In addition, we have a large network of florists, hair stylists, entertainers, musicians, caterers, venue operators, and so on. This ensures the most quality services for the best prices available.

Objectives

XYZ treats each client like royalty. Regardless of whether it is their first wedding or their tenth, every client is treated individually and with total commitment. XYZ's goal is to create a wedding and a memory that will last for years and be talked about for generations. XYZ offers different packages to meet each couple's needs, from basic packages to full-blown packages including honeymoons and beyond. XYZ is sure that their services will be in demand and net profits will increase yearly.

Mission

XYZ Wedding Consultants is a company that provides comprehensive wedding planning and services related to weddings. Our wedding consultant is experienced in providing wedding services and has training and certification in the areas of catering and wedding planning. XYZ gives each client their full attention and actively listens, then designs each wedding individually rather than working from a cookie-cutter script. XYZ creates wedding dreams. We will create the wedding according to what the client desires. If XYZ cannot create the specified wedding in the time needed, XYZ will turn the job down and recommend another qualified consultant. XYZ wants each bride to get exactly what they want and deserve and if that means they find it somewhere else then XYZ is dedicated to providing the bride and groom with that option. Included in XYZ's wedding services are weddings, honeymoons, receptions, budget planning and answers to etiquette questions.

Keys to Success

The keys to our success are as follows:

1. Service our clients' needs in a prompt and efficient manner.

2. Maintain an excellent network of vendors and professionals in the wedding business.

3. Always be courteous and professional.

Company Summary

XYZ Wedding Consultants is a new company that provides planning of weddings and unions. XYZ provides a comprehensive service and takes the stress out of wedding planning. Families can relax, enjoy the day, and know that XYZ has everything under control and has thought of every detail.

Company Ownership

XYZ is owned and operated by Sarah and Loreena Brown, its founders. As the company grows, it is the intention of the owners to register as a limited liability company or as a corporation, whichever fits the needs of the company and its owners.

Start-Up Summary

The company founders, Sarah and Loreena Brown, will handle day-to-day operations of the plan and will work collaboratively to ensure that this business venture is a success. Loreena will take care of the business and accounting and Sarah will take care of the actual wedding consulting.

The start-up costs are estimated to be $3,000. This includes any fees, logo design, or marketing needed. An additional $3,000 will be deposited in an account as operating capital for the first couple of months. Start-up costs are to be financed by a microbusiness loan already secured by the bank.

START UP	
Requirements	
Start-Up Expenses	
Legal	$200
Stationery, business cards, etc.	$450
Brochures	$450
Business insurance	$300
Research and development	$200
Expensed equipment	$900
Miscellaneous	$500
Total Start-Up Expenses	**$3,000**

START UP	
Start-Up Assets	
Cash required	$3,000
Other current assets	$0
Long-term assets	$0
Total Start-Up Assets	**$3,000**
Total Requirements	**$6,000**
Start-Up Funding	
Start-up expenses to fund	$3,000
Start-up assets to fund	$3,000
Total Funding Required	**$6,000**
Assets	
Noncash assets from start-up	$0
Cash requirements from start-up	$3,000
Additional cash raised	$0
Cash balance on starting date	$3,000
Total Assets	**$3,000**
Liabilities and Capital	
Liabilities	
Current borrowing	$0
Long-term liabilities	$0
Accounts payable (outstanding bills)	$0
Other current liabilities (interest free)	$0
Total Liabilities	$0
Capital	
Planned Investment	
SBA loan	$6,000
Additional investment requirement	$0
Total Planned Investment	**$6,000**
Loss at start-up (start-up expenses)	($3,000)
Total Capital	**$3,000**
Total Capital and Liabilities	**$3,000**
Total Funding	**$6,000**

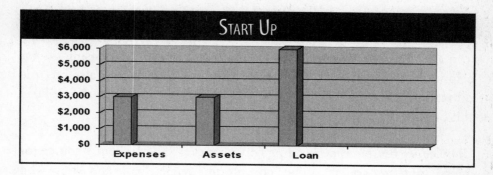

Company Locations and Facilities

This business will be a home-based business. It is set up in a home office space. This includes all the necessary equipment to run a business such as business machines, phones, and Internet access. As the company grows and becomes too large for the home office space, a larger facility may be needed.

Services

We are a comprehensive wedding consulting business and provide the following services: etiquette advice, event scheduling, the best-priced invitations and products, vendor confirmation, rehearsal attendance, supervision of both ceremony and reception setup, budget planning, booking honeymoon trips, booking music, booking caterers, floral designs, wedding venue designs, consultation on bridal dresses, bridesmaids' dresses, and grooms' and groomsmen's attire.

Market Analysis Summary

According to the Bridal Association of America's Wedding Market Summary, the number of estimated weddings in 2009 will be more than 2.3 million and the total estimated amount to be spent on those weddings will be more than $71 billion.

The bride of the 21st century spends more on this one special day in her life than any other, and the amount is only increasing as she attempts to reach perfection with her wedding day. Once reserved only for the very rich, today's brides-to-be and grooms-to-be, often busy with dual careers, yet wanting to make their wedding uniquely personal, are turning to consultants for help in reducing the stress of their wedding day. Consultants also save the couple valuable time and money by helping plan the much-anticipated day and finding the best deals for everything the couple wants.

Couples are finding that wedding consultants are an excellent resource for information and contacts. They consult on a regular basis and know who to contact for what the couple is searching for. They also have ideas and expertise from which the average bride would be able to benefit. Hiring a wedding coordinator could help ensure that the wedding day turns out to be more memorable than the bride ever could have imagined.

An average wedding using a coordinator costs about $20,000. Some coordinators charge an hourly rate ranging from $50 to $150. According to many wedding coordinators, the average wedding takes about 30 to 40 hours of coordinating, ending up earning between $1,500 and $3,000.

Creating a dream wedding requires imagination and energy, a concern for detail, and a love of organization to make certain that things run smoothly.

XYZ will help couples decide on a budget and help them stick to it. XYZ will also help them select the wedding dress; set trial hair and makeup appointments; confirm wedding day appointments; prepare and confirm wedding reception toasts or speeches; update life, house, and car insurance policies; complete change of name and change of address paperwork; open joint bank accounts (if desired); determine who will return the groom's formal attire; and arrange for a location, caterer, entertainment, wedding cake, and "going away" wardrobe.

Market Segmentation

Wedding consulting is a very rewarding business. As a consultant, we are able to transform a couple's dreams into reality. Many women will say that they had their weddings planned out since they were a little girl. With our skills, contacts, and experience we can make a fairy tale come true. Here are some other statistics from the Fairchild Bridal Group:

- 💜 This year it is estimated that 1 out of 64 women in the United States got married.

- 💜 This year there will be about 42,300 weddings every weekend in the United States.

- 💜 This year there will be about 17 million bridesmaids and groomsmen.

- 💜 Finally, this year there will be about 287 million wedding guests.

A client segment to consider is the family members and guests attending weddings, anniversaries, and similar events. This segment requires event preparation services like gift ideas, etiquette tips, and so on.

Couples are waiting longer to get married. Demographically, couples are waiting until the ages of 27 to 29, and this will be the target population. In the area that XYZ serves, there is a large population of couples at this age.

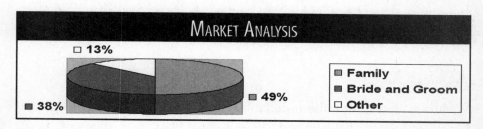

MARKET ANALYSIS							
		2003	2003	2005	2006	2007	
Potential Customers	Growth						CAGR
Brides and Grooms	5.0%	1,500	1,575	1,654	1,737	1,824	5.01%
Family Members	5.0%	5,000	5,250	5,513	5,789	6,078	5.00%
Other	5.0%	1,000	1,050	1,103	1,158	1,216	5.01%
Total	5.0%	7,500	7,875	8,270	8,684	9,118	5.00%

MARKET ANALYSIS

* CAGR - Compound Annual growth Rate is the year-over-year growth rate for an investment over a specified period of time. The compound annual growth rate is calculated by taking the nth roote of the total percentage growth rate, where n is the number of years in the period being considered.

$$CAGR = \left(\frac{\text{Ending Value}}{\text{Beginning Value}} \right)^{(1 \, + \, \# \text{ of years})} -1$$

Target Market Segment Strategy

XYZ Wedding Consultants will offer its services mostly to the brides and grooms, as well as to the family members. XYZ will offer itself as an experienced provider of wedding planning services. XYZ will be offering a comprehensive, full range of services and this will provide clients with a one-stop-shopping experience that is different from competitors. This one-stop service will provide clients more time for making personal preparations for their wedding, with the peace of mind that they are being taken care of. The network of vendors and suppliers that XYZ has enables XYZ to offer the most competitive prices available in the area for about every product and service that a bride and groom may need. The savings that XYZ offers will enable clients to justify the cost of using a wedding consultant.

Market Needs

Weddings are a multimillion-dollar business. In 2006, the Fairchild Bridal Group estimated that about $125 million dollars were spent on about 2.1 million weddings. The cost of weddings, like many other things, has inflated drastically over the years. Where it used to be just the bride's family that was funding events, now it is the bride, groom, and both of their families. That is as many as six wage earners as opposed to relying on the wage on the bride's father.

There has been a 73 percent increase in the cost of a wedding in the past 15 years, according to the Fairchild Bridal Group. They estimate that the average cost of a wedding is now about $30,000. The bridal industry now encompasses a greater venue than it used to. It includes travel, home decorations, home furnishings and much more.

A bride, even though she does not have the time, still wants to have the same type of weddings brides wanted in the past and more. Although both major customer segments — brides and grooms and family members — plan and budget for the wedding ceremony as far as a year or more in advance, they often realize that they cannot make all the necessary preparations by themselves. They seek outside sources, in this case a wedding consultant, to fill in the gaps. Professional women know the value of their time and they know the value of outsourcing when they do not have the time to do it themselves. This creates a huge need for wedding consultants.

Service Business Analysis

There are a number of other wedding planning agencies that may provide services such as catering connections or a hair stylist. XYZ is different in that it provides multiple services with literally hundreds of different vendors to choose from. This comprehensive service sets XYZ apart from its competition and creates the chance of decent revenue for wedding consulting services. In addition, Sarah and Loreena have had years of experience in different areas such as fashion, catering, and wedding consulting.

Competition and Buying Patterns

Competitive analysis conducted by the company owners has shown that there are 25 companies currently offering some sort of wedding planning services in the Hickory, North Carolina area. The majority of the competitors offer only a limited line of services such as catering, flower arrangements, or gifts. Of these competitors, only two offer a greater number of services like those offered by XYZ. The following is the list of the major competitors with a brief description of their services:

♥ **Picture Perfect Planning** — Offers a variety of "bride" and "bachelorette" apparel as well as various displays of the latest trends and fashions for parties and events.

♥ **Charlotte Arrangements** — This company was founded in 1994 with the goal of delivering outstanding results to its clients by producing impeccable events with flawless execution. It claims to be the region's premier destination management and event planning production company. They offer the most comprehensive in-house services for events, transportation, tours, destination management, convention services, meetings, and team-building programs.

♥ **The Cat's Meow Complete** — They offer planning services for weddings. They state that they have teamed with the most reliable and professional vendors in the area. They offer planning packages or one-day only services to suit any theme or budget.

The market research has also shown that customers anticipate the complete wedding consulting services to be expensive and they budget accordingly. In fact, lower prices are very often associated with poor-quality service. By aggregating a complete range of wedding services under one roof, XYZ Wedding Consultants will offer its customers the ease of one-stop shopping.

Strategy and Implementation Summary

XYZ has a simple strategy, and that is to provide clients with a wide range of services custom tailored to their individual needs. Therefore, whether they require a complete package or simply consulting on a particular service, XYZ can help.

Competitive Edge

Because XYZ has a whole cast of vendors they do work with, they can offer their clients the ease of one-stop shopping. XYZ will leverage its consultant's expertise in planning such events to competitively position itself as a premier provider of wedding services. Both owners have very strong communication skills that will help get the word out that XYZ offers the highest-quality services in the wedding industry.

Sales Strategy

The company's sales strategy will be based on the following elements:

- ♥ Two-inch-by-three-inch ads describing the services will be placed in the local Yellow Pages.

- ♥ Placing advertisements in the local press, including *Hickory Daily News*, the *Charlotte Observer*, and the *Taylorsville Times*.

- ♥ Continue to develop affiliate relationships with other service providers (florists, hair stylists, caterers) that would receive a percentage of sales to the referred customers.

- ♥ Finally, word-of-mouth referrals will be created as more weddings are performed. Business cards will be handed out at these events upon request.

SALES FORECAST			
	2007	2008	2009
Brides and Grooms	$54,200	$65,040	$71,544
Family Members	$25,800	$30,960	$34,056
Other	$15,300	$18,360	$20,196
Total Sales	$95,300	$114,360	$125,796
Other	$0	$0	$0

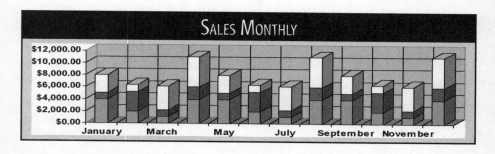

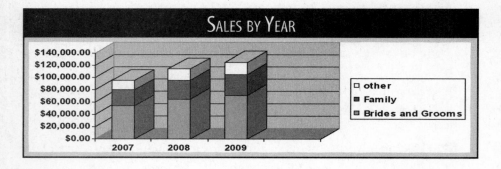

Management Summary

Our wedding consultant is Sarah Brown. Loreena Brown is the business manager. Collectively, they have planned and serviced over 300 weddings and receptions. They are knowledgeable about all areas of planning, decorating, as well as budgeting. Sarah has a Bachelor of Science (B.S.) in hospitality management and a minor in interior design. She has been a wedding consultant for over four years and became interested in providing consultant services when she successfully planned her first few weddings for family and friends. Since then, Sarah has received her certification in wedding planning from the National Association of Wedding Consultants (NAWC) and Professional Wedding Planners. Loreena has a Masters of Business Administration (MBA) and a B.S. in interior decorating and design. Loreena also received her certification from the NAWC and has been a wedding planner for three years. Sarah enjoys all aspects of planning traditional and nontraditional weddings. Loreena enjoys working in the background with the numbers and money.

Personnel Plan

Initially, XYZ Wedding Consultants' personnel will include only the two owners, both of whom will be working full time. As the personnel plan shows, we expect to hire an additional wedding consultant in the next two years. This person will work full time, but will not be included in the management decisions.

PERSONNEL PLAN			
	2007	2008	2009
Owner	$53,100	$76,200	$85,800
Other	$0	$0	$20,000
Total People	0	0	0
Total Payroll	$53,100	$76,200	$105,800

Financial Plan

The following subtopics represent the financial plan of XYZ Wedding Consultants.

GENERAL ASSUMPTIONS			
	2007	2008	2009
Plan Month	1	2	3
Current Interest Rate	10.00%	10.00%	10.00%
Long-term Interest Rate	10.00%	10.00%	10.00%
Tax Rate	25.42%	25.00%	25.42%
Other	0	0	0

Break-Even Analysis

The following table and chart summarize our break-even analysis.

BREAK-EVEN ANALYSIS	
Monthly Revenue Break-Even	$5,486
Assumptions:	
Average Percent Variable Cost	0%
Estimated Monthly Fixed Cost	$5,486

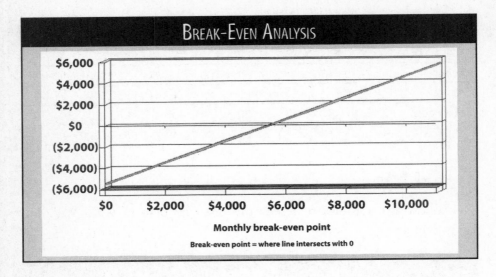

BREAK-EVEN ANALYSIS

Monthly break-even point

Break-even point = where line intersects with 0

Projected Profit and Loss

Our projected profit and loss is shown in the following table:

PRO FORMA PROFIT AND LOSS			
	2007	2008	2009
Sales	$95,300	$114,360	$125,796
Direct cost of sales	$0	$0	$0
Other	$0	$0	$0
Total cost of sales	$0	$0	$0
Gross margin	$95,300	$114,360	$125,796
Gross margin %	100.00%	100.00%	100.00%
Expenses			
Payroll	$53,100	$76,200	$1005,800
Sales and marketing and other expenses	$4,550	$1,000	$2,000
Depreciation	$0	$0	$0
Leased equipment	$0	$0	$0
Utilities	$0	$0	$0
Insurance	$0	$0	$0
Rent	$0	$0	$0
Payroll taxes	$7,965	$11,430	$12,870

PRO FORMA PROFIT AND LOSS			
Other	$0	$0	$0
Total operating expenses	$65,615	$88,630	$100,670
Profit before interest and taxes	$29,685	$25,730	$25,126
EBITDA*	$29,685	$25,730	$25,126
Interest expense	$0	$0	$0
Taxes incurred	$7,421	$6,433	$6,386
Net profit	$22,264	$19,298	$18,740
Net profit/sales	23.36%	16.87%	14.90%

* EBITDA = Earnings before interest, taxes, depreciation, and amortization

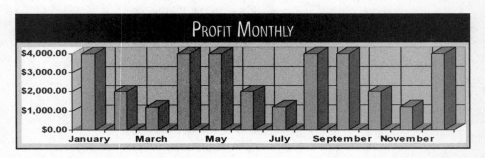

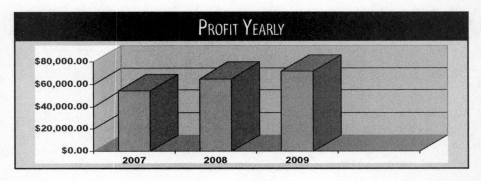

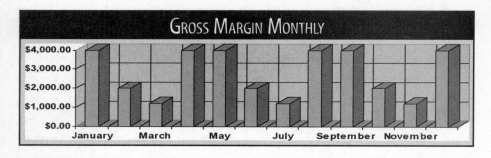

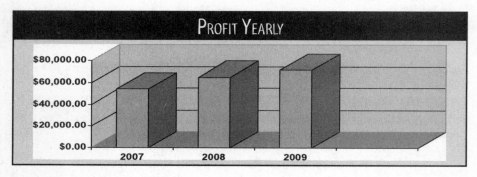

Projected Cash Flow

The following chart and table show our cash flow projections:

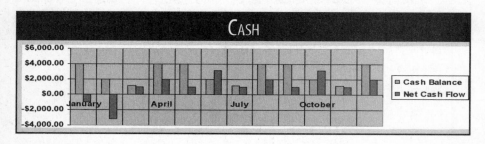

CASH FLOW			
	2007	2008	2009
Cash received			
Cash from operations			

CASH FLOW			
	2007	2008	2009
Cash sales	$38,120	$45,744	$50,318
Cash from receivables	$45,494	$66,279	$74,075
Subtotal cash from operations	$83,614	$112,023	$124,383
Additional cash received			
Sales tax, VAT, HST/GST received	$0	$0	$0
New current borrowing	$0	$0	$0
New other liabilities (interest-free)	$0	$0	$0
New long-term liabilities	$0	$0	$0
Sales of other current assets	$0	$0	$0
Sales of long-term assets	$0	$0	$0
New investments received	$0	$0	$0
Subtotal cash received	$83,614	$112,023	$124,383
Expenditures			
Expenditures from operations			
Cash spending	$53,100	$76,200	$85,800
Bill payments	$18,072	$19,177	$21,059
Subtotal spent on operations	$71,172	$95,377	$106,859
Additional cash spent			
Sales tax, VAT, HST/GST paid out	$0	$0	$0
Principal repayment of current borrowing	$0	$0	$0
Other liabilities' principal repayment	$0	$0	$0
Long-term liabilities' principal repayment	$0	$0	$0
Purchase other current assets	$0	$0	$0
Purchase long-term assets	$0	$0	$0
Dividends	$0	$0	$0
Subtotal cash spent	$71,172	$95,377	$106,859
Net cash flow	$12,442	$16,646	$17,534
Cash balance	$17,442	$34,088	$52,623

As a wedding consultant, you will be called upon to create menus for your brides. These can be as simple as some finger foods or a hundred pizzas. Many brides want fancier affairs that include multicourse meals. Below are some sample menus that wedding consultants have used for their brides. Most of the time you will leave the cooking and work to a caterer, but you will be called upon to negotiate and create the menu based upon the wishes of the bridal party.

BUFFET-STYLE MENU

Tossed Salad with Raspberry Vinaigrette

Traditional Caesar Salad

Choice of One:

Baked Manicotti

Mostaccioli

Choice of Two:

Baked Ham

Sirloin Beef

Baked Chicken

BUFFET-STYLE MENU

Roast Sirloin

Chicken Piccata

Choice of One:

Glazed Baby Carrots

Green Beans Almondine

Fresh Vegetables

Choice of One:

Garlic Mashed Potatoes

Classic Mashed Potatoes

Twice-Baked Potatoes

Choice of One:

Chocolate Mousse

Vanilla Ice Cream

Mini Cheesecakes

Rolls/Croissants

STATION MENU

Antipasto Display

Features: Olives, Marinated Vegetables, Smoked Mozzarella, Rolled Salami, Tuscan Peppers, and Marinated Artichoke Hearts in a Red Wine Vinaigrette

Fresh Fruit Presentation

Sliced American and Tropical Fruits and Berries with Honey Poppyseed Yogurt Dip and Chocolate Fondue

Passed Butler Style on Silver Trays with Fresh Cut Flowers

With White Glove Service / Kindly Select Four

Almond Crusted Shrimp with Dutch Curry Sauce — Oysters Bienville

STATION MENU

Barbecue Gulf Shrimp — Carolina Crab Cakes with Cajun Remoulade

Blue Crab Stuffed Mushrooms

Chicken Beggar's Purse and Wild Mushrooms — Beef and Mushroom Duxelles en Croute

Baked Brie en Croute — Petite Quiche

Carving Station — Pick Two

Prime Rib

Served with Peppercorn Demi-Glace and Horseradish Cream

Basket of Silver Dollar Rolls

or

Roast Breast of Turkey

Served with Giblet Gravy and Cranberry Relish

Appropriate Condiments

Silver Dollar Rolls

or

Bourbon-Glazed Ham

Served with Mustard and Sweet Pickle Relish

Silver Dollar Rolls

Pasta Station

Tortellini, Fusilli, and Penne Pastas Prepared with a Selection of Bay Shrimp, Diced Ham, Tomatoes, Bell Peppers, Wild Mushrooms, and Pancetta

Creamy Chive and Clam Sauce, Marinara, and Pesto Sauces

Freshly Cracked Pepper and Grated Parmesan Cheese

Complemented with Garlic Bread or Bread Sticks

Dessert Station

Wedding Cake

Assorted Cookies and Pastries

Cheesecake

PLATED DINNER

Appetizer — Select One

Lobster Bisque with Cilantro Croutons

Napoleon of Fresh Mozzarella and Tomato Drizzled with Balsamic Vinaigrette

Pan-Seared Crabmeat Cake with Leek Julienne and Pesto Oil

Salads — Select One

Boston Bibb with Hearts of Palm, Roma Tomatoes, and Bermuda Onion, Served with a Raspberry Vinaigrette

Caesar Salad with Garlic Croutons and Asiago Cheese

Spinich Salad with Enoki Mushrooms, Sliced Onions, and Plum Tomatoes

Served with a Sour Cream Bacon Dressing

Entrees — Select One

Roasted Duck Breast

with Merlot Thyme Jelly

Chicken Forestiere

Sauteed Boneless Breast of Chicken with Garlic, Shallots, and Wild Mushrooms with Madeira Wine Sauce

New York Strip Loin

Broiled with a Pinot Noir Demi-Glace

Grilled Wild Salmon

Wild Northwest Salmon with Sherry and Morel Mushroom Cream

Desserts — Select One

Cheesecake

Tiramisu

Seating Arrangements

Appendix D

One of the hardest things to do as a wedding consultant is to be able to look at a room and envision in your mind what it will look like on a wedding day. This may be easier if you use a certain venue often. You have to figure out where decorations will go, where tables will be placed, and where the food will be set up. The bride may have some requests about where people sit. You will have to figure out how to fit the number of people the bride plans on inviting and even make a decision of whether or not it will work. There are certain laws of physics that have to be considered.

One of the best tools that a wedding consultant can create is a floor plan. This gives you a blueprint of how to set up for a wedding or reception. This also gives a visual instrument which you can use with the bride to make sure you have everything set up correctly before you start moving chairs and tables. Included here are some actual samples of floor plans that have been used by wedding consultants.

FLOOR PLAN 1

CHAIRS SET UP ALONG WALL

Glass Windows / Terrace
Entrance from Outside

PUNCH, SODA, & WATER TABLE
IF NOT THEN PUNCH FOUNTAIN

HORS
D'OEUVRES
TABLE

MANY TABLES
AGAINST EACH OTHER

PEOPLE CAN MOVE
DOWN EITHER SIDE OF
THE BUFFET

ENTRANCE TO BALL ROOM

CHAIRS SET UP ALONG WALL

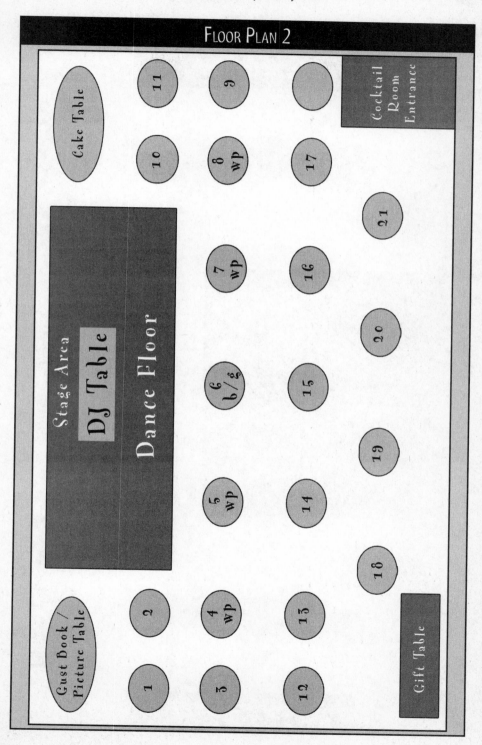

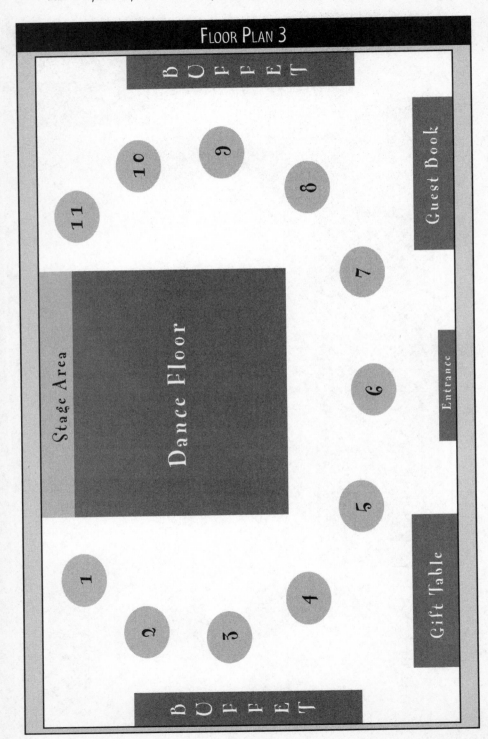

Bibliography

BPlans.com. "Wedding Consultant Business Plan." **http://www.bplans. com/sample_business_plans/Wedding_and_Event_Planning_ Business_Plans/Wedding_Consultant_Business_Plan/executive_ summary_fc.cfm**.

Fairchild Bridal Group. Fairchild Infobank American Wedding Study, 2002.

Peters, A.J. and Entrepreneur Press. *Start Your Own Wedding Consultant Business*. 2nd ed. Irvine, Calif.: Entrepreneur Press, 2007.

Pinson, L. and Jinnett, J. *Steps to Small Business Start-Up: Everything You Need to Know to Turn Your Idea Into a Successful Business*. Chicago: Kaplan, 2006.

PowerHomeBiz.com. "Earn Money as a Professional Wedding Coordinator." **http://www.powerhomebiz.com/vol26/wedding.htm**.

Sandlin, E.F. and Entrepreneur Press. *Start Your Own Wedding Consultant Business*. Irvine, Calif.: Entrepreneur Press, 2003.

Sell the Bride. **http://www.sellthebride.com/tipsstats.html**.

Sitarz, D. *Sole Proprietorship: Small Business Start-Up Kit.* 2nd ed. Carbondale, Ill.: Nova, 2005.

Socrates (editors). *Building a Successful Business Plan: Advice From the Experts.* Chicago: Socrates Media, 2006.

Turner, K.T. and Entrepreneur Press. *Start Your Own Event Planning Business.* Irvine, Calif.: Entrepreneur Press, 2004.

Biography

Author

J ohn N Peragine, Ph.D. was born in Miami, Florida, in 1970. He grew up in the Tampa Bay area, but attended the North Carolina School of the Arts, in Winston Salem, for high school. He attended Florida State University and earned a bachelor's degree in psychology from Appalachian State University. He finished his master's degree and Ph.D. in Natural Health at Clayton College of Natural Health in spring 2002. In August 2007, he took the plunge. John had been a social worker in child protective services for far too many years, but had been toying with the idea of being a writer. He had written for a few national magazines and received positive responses for his work. He decided to quit social work and took a chance at writing full time. Luck was on his side, as during his first year, he was assigned to write seven books for Atlantic Publishing Group, Inc. Since then, he has completed numerous freelance projects, including writing for magazines, and creating workbooks, eBooks, articles, ghost-written books, blogs, and more. He is now working full-time and hopes to get fiction completed and published soon. More information can be found at **http://johnperagine. books.officelive.com**.

Index

A

Advertising 44, 45, 60, 66, 67, 68, 74, 79, 88, 93, 105, 107, 116-118, 132, 174, 177, 201, 236, 242
Arrangement 64, 168
Association 44, 75, 76, 109, 110

B

Benefit 29, 55, 69, 75, 77, 139, 151, 175, 230, 260
Best Man 220
Blog 116, 117, 224
Booth 44, 65, 66, 118, 119, 120, 121-125
Bridal 23, 44, 66, 72, 91, 106,-109, 118-122, 125, 126, 185, 223, 226, 228, 238, 245-254, 259, 263, 273
Bride 23, 25, 26, 29, 30, 32, 39, 42, 45, 49, 65, 71, 72, 75, 78, 79, 92, 93, 103, 104, 106, 107, 108, 112, 114, 116, 123, 130, 131, 135, 173, 174, 176, 192, 198, 215, 216, 219-223, 225, 227, 230, 231, 236- 241, 243, 255, 256, 259, 260, 262, 263, 277
Brochure 114-116, 126, 132, 177
Budget 21, 23, 29, 36, 39, 42, 44, 58, 72, 73, 93, 98, 99, 104, 105, 108, 120, 121, 126, 165, 177, 190, 222, 224, 255, 256, 259, 260, 263, 264
Business 2, 21, 23- 25, 27-29, 33-38, 40, 42-47, 50-53, 57, 58, 60-65, 67-69, 74-78, 81-88, 90-111, 113, 114, 116, 122-127, 131-134, 137, 138, 140-142, 144, 146-154, 158, 161-163, 167, 173-178, 180-189, 191-201, 203, 205-207, 209-213, 215-219, 221-226, 228-230, 236, 237, 239, 242, 243, 256, 257,

259, 260, 262, 266, 281

C

Cake 21, 49, 65, 75, 138, 226, 239, 260
Card 116, 123, 126, 146, 168, 180, 188
Caterer 21, 26, 41, 75, 152, 228, 260, 273
CD 1, 2, 10, 37, 83, 123, 124, 145, 182
Commercial 71
Community 10, 111
Competitor 77, 78
Computer 70, 71, 101, 179, 223, 224, 229, 237, 242, 243
Conservative 89
Consultant 2, 21, 24-26, 29-39, 41, 46, 49, 50, 52, 56, 60, 61, 63, 68, 75-79, 90, 92, 94, 96, 99, 101, 103-105, 108-110, 112, 114, 119, 121, 127, 129, 131, 132, 135, 138, 144, 154, 163, 164, 174, 191, 209, 215-220, 222, 224-226, 229, 230, 237, 239, 243, 255, 256, 260, 262-264, 266, 273, 277
Coordinator 29, 225, 226, 230, 240, 242, 260
Corporation 64, 139, 257

D

Dress 67

E

Emergency 121, 181, 200, 223, 225-227, 229-231, 237, 239, 240
Entertainment 21, 29, 130, 260
Expenses 36-39, 47, 48, 68, 72, 73, 131, 134, 144, 150, 152-154, 177, 195, 200, 207, 208, 212, 236, 258, 268, 269
Experience 25, 29, 35, 39, 51, 52, 76, 93, 99, 120, 126, 133, 148, 167, 175, 177, 192, 196, 201, 225, 228-230, 261, 262, 263

F

Family 23, 26, 29, 34, 36, 39, 42, 46, 49, 50, 52, 79, 93, 116, 121, 124, 147, 162, 174, 189, 190, 192, 201, 210, 219, 222, 228-230, 236, 242, 243, 261, 262, 263, 266
Finance 92
Florist 66, 70, 198
Forms 87, 99, 102, 137, 139, 140, 141, 154, 156, 158, 161, 162, 163, 202, 209

G

Gas 73, 101
Gift 49, 50, 261
Groom 21, 23, 30, 42, 75, 93, 219, 222, 225, 227, 231, 240, 241, 243, 256, 260, 262

H

Hardware 123
Hobby 37, 42, 110, 147, 148, 228

I

Independent 27, 143, 144, 145
Industry 2, 23, 44, 51, 59-62, 75,
   76, 84, 87, 88, 92, 97, 99,
   100, 105, 107, 108, 181,
   182, 185, 205, 211, 212,
   218, 222, 236, 263, 264
Internet 2, 7, 34, 42, 43, 48, 55,
   56, 57, 93, 101, 109, 113,
   118, 132, 135, 146, 208,
   221, 223, 237, 259

L

Letterhead 58
Loan 46, 47, 92, 257, 258
Location 21, 71, 72, 85, 109, 118,
   119, 120, 130, 150, 163,
   174, 238, 260
Logo 93, 115, 119, 134, 135,
   180, 257

M

Magazine 108
Mailing 56, 57, 58, 65, 123, 125,
   126, 189
Maintenance 73
Market 24, 36, 42, 47, 53, 56- 58,
   60, 61, 63, 76, 82, 83, 87-
   93, 95, 100, 104, 108, 131,
   149, 152, 153, 185, 201,
   211, 213, 224, 237, 239,
   264
Membership 72, 132
Money 24, 32, 35, 36, 38, 40-42,
   45-48, 58, 62-64, 68, 78, 82,
   83, 92, 102-105, 115, 118-
   120, 123, 124, 129, 131,
   133, 134, 140, 141, 154,
   164, 175, 179, 180, 191,
   194-196, 199, 200, 202,
   204, 218, 237, 239, 242,
   243, 260, 266
Music 29, 30, 65, 119, 215, 216,
   220, 240, 259

N

Newsletters 10, 114, 120
Newspaper 89, 97, 113, 117, 135,
   226, 246
Niche 40, 61, 77, 78, 92
Notary 202, 204, 206

O

Opportunity 28, 44, 95, 98, 99,
   105, 186, 215, 224, 237
Organize 37, 76, 106

P

Pictures 56, 65, 106, 121, 123,
   237
Planning 2, 5, 24, 25, 26, 30, 35,
   41, 43, 44, 49, 50, 60, 63,
   65, 72, 74, 81, 86, 88, 90,
   102, 108, 111, 112, 114,
   121, 126, 129, 130, 134,
   135, 138, 139, 167, 194,
   198, 201, 215, 221, 222,
   224, 227-230, 236, 238-240,
   242, 243, 255- 257, 259,
   262, 263, 264, 266
Print 46, 58, 70, 112
Privacy 146
Public 34, 45, 97, 114, 133, 201

R

Registration 123

S

Schedule 38, 52, 70, 105, 114, 154, 158, 166, 174, 176, 199, 222, 223, 238
Seating 16, 277
Service 9, 12, 15, 39, 92, 100, 110, 163, 164, 165, 169, 208, 256, 263, 274

T

Tax 64, 69, 73, 102, 105, 137-142, 145, 147, 150-158, 161, 198, 202, 229, 271
Threats 181, 187
Travel 23, 36, 68, 69, 70, 71, 72, 73, 195, 238, 239, 263

V

Vehicle 73
Vendor 64, 78, 106, 116, 133, 134, 165, 168, 202, 204, 226, 236, 238, 239, 242, 259

Video 122, 149

W

Web 2, 7, 12, 34, 40, 43, 45, 55, 56, 59, 92, 93, 108, 117, 119, 131, 140, 149, 162, 168, 177-180, 189, 212, 221, 224, 226, 236, 237, 238
Wedding 2, 21, 23-47, 49-52, 55-58, 60,-66, 68, 71, 72, 74-79, 8-92, 94-116, 118, 119, 121-124, 126, 127, 129-135, 138, 142, 144, 146-151, 153, 154, 158, 161, 164, 165, 168, 173-177, 179, 182, 184-187, 189-192, 194-196, 198, 200-202, 205, 209-211, 213, 215-230, 236-240, 242, 243, 247, 249, 250, 254-257, 259-264, 266, 273, 277, 281